W9-DIW-845

MEDITATION AND THE ART OF DYING

Pandit
Usharbudh Arya, Ph.D.

Published by

HIMALAYAN INTERNATIONAL INSTITUTE
OF YOGA SCIENCE AND PHILOSOPHY
Honesdale, Pennsylvania

॥ यस्यच्छाया ऽमृतं यस्य मृत्युः

कस्मै देवाय हविषा विधेम ॥

मृत्योर्मा अमृतं गमय

Surrender

Shri Guru, my master
Raise me from this fearsome worldly cycle
Of entering a womb, becoming a fetus, being born,
getting old and dying.
Save me through self-realization.
Having given reassurance to all beings,
I have come to your feet,
Master of yogis,
Save me.

Detached from all things,
Tranquil, expert in all sciences,
Remover of all doubts, ever intent
Is my king of gurus.
Save me, Guru, from the burning fire of the world,
For I am scorched and bitten by the serpent of Time.
I have now come seeking refuge with you.
From this day I shall hurt no living beings with acts,
mind or speech.
I take this great vow.
Bitten by the black serpent of ignorance,
Suffering from its poison,
Ready to die,
I beg you, revive me with a portion of the amrta of your words.

(I am) burning under the sun of worldly existence,
Scorched in the body and mind,
Sprinkle me with the waters of your word of wisdom.

These words are addressed to the Guru by a disciple when seeking vows of
Swamihood.

Contents

Introduction   vii

Death in Western Spirituality   1

Birth and Death: Cycles   20

Why Grieve over the Body?   43

Actions and Transitions   69

Immortality of the Masters   100

Conquest of Death   124

The Yoga of Dissolution   147

Conclusion   173

Acknowledgments

In presenting this humble work to the readers, I falsely take credit for the meritorious deeds of those who spent much labor in transcribing from lecture tapes, editing, typing, retyping and finally prepared the volume. My special thanks are due to Mary Gail Peterson Sovik of the Meditation Center Ashram and her team of the Center members, especially Kathy Trovecke. I am also grateful to Professor Ronald Neuhaus, Brandt Dayton and Dr. Rudolph M. Ballentine for all the editorial suggestions that have enhanced the value of the present work. May they know Brahman in this very life.

Introduction

Death is not a process apart from being born and living; it is included in birth and life. As Carlisle said, an author has the right to call black white so long as he is consistent with it. I will refer to the process of birth, new birth, rebirth by the term "death," only to follow the general convention.

There are many kinds of death. One, the process of constantly dying and regenerating our bodies. Some years ago my eldest daughter, Sushumna, burned her hand by spilling scalded milk on it. Our doctor at the hospital, whom she had to visit repeatedly, was a member of the Meditation Center. Later, as some dead flesh was peeling off her arm, the doctor said that that part of the skin was always changing in us. That is what we leave as the ring around the bath rub—so many dead cells.

This we can easily call the process of continuous "reincarnation," new flesh being created to replace the old one that we shed constantly. We never have the same body with which we were born. We may give this process the name of cellular death.

Two, the final termination of the body when the cells no longer regenerate and the light of the spirit must abandon its accustomed home. For those who have lived in attachment to their flesh, this death is involuntary and the fear of it is very painful. They have no control over the dying process because they had exercised very little discipline during the life-process. This is the way most of us die, clinging and crying pitifully.

Three, there is the practice of daily meditation in which initial glimpses of the face of death occur, somewhat vaguely. Our daily meditation is a withdrawal of senses, a spiritual awareness in which the body consciousness gradually dissolves. It is as though minute doses of this daily death innoculate us against the larger plague. As the meditator advances in his practice he learns to control the processes of dying. He is not yet liberated, and bound to the karmic process he must yield to the hour of death, he has developed a certain control whereby he may direct his *pranas*, the vital forces, to leave the body in the manner of an expert. Such a person dies in meditation, often guided by a Master.

Four, in order to be so guided in the death process the disciple is sometimes prepared many years or decades in advance through a *diksha-mrtyu*, initiatory death, which is an experience received by a few through the Master's grace. Such an initiation into death is the beginning of a new spiritual life. In fact, until we die at the Master's hand, we cannot begin to live spiritually. Here, the narrative of my father's guru may clarify the point.

My father's guru was born in a Muslim family and became a judge in British India, which was very rare at that time. He used to go out hunting with the British judges and officers. One day this arrogant man, a man of high power and position, went out hunting with his friends. While returning they got lost and were very thirsty. They rode their horses toward a hut, climbed down, asked for and received some water given to them by an old Brahmin. (Brahmins are philosophers who perform priestly functions.) Having quenched their thirst, they mounted their horses and were preparing to leave. But when the Muslim judge mounted his horse, the Brahmin looked him straight in the eye and said, "You cannot go!"

"Who is this man?" thought the high court judge. "Here is a little man with a sheet wrapped around a bag of bones, living in a little hut. I just took a drink of water from him and he tells me I can't go!"

But there was something compelling in the Brahmin's glance so the judge dismounted. He told all his colleagues to go on without him, and that he would return later. The Brahmin hermit took him by the hand, led him into the hut, and before he knew what was happening, he saw his own body all in pieces, lying around scattered. A leg here, head there, arms elsewhere. He saw that body lying strewn and scattered, limb by limb, just for a few moments. Then every limb was put back together again. This is called initiatory death. The Brahmin looked at him and said, "You were a great Brahmin philosopher in the past life; what are you doing with this gun? Remember yourself! Now you may return home."

The judge, very surprised and astonished, mounted

his horse and went away. After that incident, he refused to go hunting with his friends. He stopped drinking and eating meat. The moment he finished his daily work, he rode out to see the hermit. For six months he did that, and was trained into meditation. He withdrew from life, renounced everything, and took the name Shivananda Swami. (Not to be confused with the Shivananda of Rishikesh.) He went away and lived in the desert for the rest of his life. People came to him to receive high yoga initiations. My father received his initiation from this man.

This initiatory death is a conscious process in yoga whereby a hale and hearty person may experience death for a little while. Not everyone can withstand it. But those few who are given that kind of initiation under the power of a guru, who can alter the disciple's states of consciousness, are never the same again. The meaning of life and death completely changes for them.

Five, there is the death of a Master, like the Buddha and the other enlightened ones, those who have risen above the karmic process. The body is their instrument totally.

In ordinary terms death is generally understood as "a passing away" of a body, someone who was there but is no more. He was alive, but now is dead, ready to be buried, and that is the end. This is only a minor part of the death process however. Let us extend the definition of death to include ideas of freedom, rebirth and liberation: death as a gateway to infinity, an opening into eternity. In order to understand death as only a part of life, birth, passing away, rebirth, and so on, we have to develop a certain attitude throughout life. We have to understand the fear of death. Where does this fear come from?

The yoga technical word for fear of death is *abhinivesha*, a state of being completely possessed with body-consciousness so that death appears to be a terrible wrenching process. It is as though one's essence is being pulled away from the physical identity that is mistaken to be the self. In the Sankhya system this *abhinivesha* is one of the five hells, *andha-tamisra*, that of the darkest night. In Patanjali's system it is one of the five kleshas, afflictions and stains on the mind which begin with *avidya*, ignorance, at the head of the list. *Avidya* is fourfold: mistaking the impermanent, impure, painful and non-self for permanent, pure, pleasant and the self; the body mistaken for the spirit and the spirit mistaken for the body causes the attachment leading to the fear of death. It is in the field of ignorance that the tree of death grows.

It is not strange that the learned and the fool equally suffer the pangs of the fear of death. Each one wishes: "May I not cease to be." This fear is a natural effect of the hidden memory of the experience of the death of one's last body in the previous incarnation.

> Those who talk of death,
> sing of death,
> meditate on death,
> do not die
> and commit no suicides;
> immortals they,
> *mrityunjaya brahmacharins*
> death-conquerors, walking in God.
>
> Their moment-to-moment deaths,
> little doses of death-serum,
> make them immune;
> they have mastered
> the art of dying
> by themselves

thus being reborn,
refreshing each cell
with vital life fluid;
they are not graveyards
of dead cells.

Dying by choice
from day to day
they are not dragged
into death's snare
by force
pitifully crying
Sons of *Amrit Jyoti*
and they live
(while they live)
more than others,
if not longer.

Then there are those
who cling to life;
they do not welcome death with a smile,
nor surrender to His Will,
nor do they drop
gently, gracefully
as a dancer,
to surrender
and dissolve!

But they struggle
fight in vain,
lose by clinging;
and have not learned
the art of gaining
just by losing.

While they live
they live less,
even if longer.

This book can only be an introduction to the
Immortal Light of the death-conquering yogis. Much of
the yoga view can be learned only through a deep spiritual
experience. For thousands of years great realized beings
have communicated their inner experience in a variety of
languages and symbols.

Death in Western Spirituality

Solon, the Greek lawgiver, traveled widely. According to Herodotus, the historian, Emperor Croesus entertained Solon hospitably in his palace and asked him, "Well, my Athenian friend, I have heard a great deal about your wisdom and how widely you have traveled in the pursuit of knowledge. I cannot resist my desire to ask you a question. Who is the happiest man you have ever seen?"

Solon replied, "An Athenian called Tellus."

Emperor Croesus had expected to be told that he, himself, was the happiest man and objected to Solon's answer.

Solon replied, "My Lord . . . you are very rich, and you rule a numerous people; but the question you asked me I will not answer until I know that you have died happily . . . Though the rich have the means to satisfy their appetites and to bear calamities, and the poor have not, the poor, if they are lucky, are more likely to keep clear of trouble, and will have besides the blessings of a sound body, health, freedom from trouble, fine children and good looks. Now if a man thus favored dies as he has lived, he will be just the one you are looking for, the only sort of person who deserves to be called happy. But mark this. Until he is dead, keep the word happy in reserve. Till then he is not happy, but only lucky . . . Look to the end, no matter what it is you are considering."[1]

In other words, the success of life cannot be measured while the person is still in the process of life. Only by the way he ends his life will we know whether it has been successful. Death is the measure of life. By the way we die, we know whether we have had a good life, a happy life, a fulfilling life, a complete life; death is the culmination, the apex, the final end. The rest are all means. And so, we should make our life a preparation for that death.

Socrates, the greatest Western philosopher, with the possible exception of Pythagoras about whom so little is known, borrowed a great deal from the philosophy of the Stoics, whose thought, in turn, parallels that of the East, as reflected in such writings as the Bhagavad Gita. Plato and Aristotle were Socrates' philosophical disciples. They were not his biographers. His most inspired biographer was Xenophon. Xenophon's life of Socrates echoes the writings of the ancient East, such as the Gita when it describes the philosopher's character. Xenophon says:

> Socrates was, as I have described him, so devout that he never did anything without the sanction of the gods; so upright that he never did the smallest harm to anybody, but conferred the greatest benefits upon those who associated with him; so self-disciplined that he never chose the more pleasant course instead of the better; so judicious that he never made a mistake in deciding between better and worse; and needed

no advice, but was self-sufficient for such decisions,
capable of stating and distinguishing such alternatives
and capable both of otherwise appraising and of ex-
posing errors and encouraging towards goodness and
excellence of body and mind."[2]

So also was his death exemplary of the best traditions of East and West: Socrates had been brought to
court accused of corrupting the youth of Athens with his
philosophy, for which crime he had been sentenced to
death. It happened to be a holy month during which some
offerings were sent to the temple of the oracles of Delphus.
Until the ship carrying the offerings returned no one was
to be killed in Athens. So Socrates had to remain in chains
for a whole month. His disciples, who were powerful
people, offered to help him escape. But he refused, saying,
"All my life I've taught respect for the laws."

During this period he held the dialogues with Crito
and Phaedo. The *Phaedo* begins with Echecrates, an
admirer of Socrates, questioning Phaedo as to how the
condemned philosopher had spent his final hours in prison
before his execution. Phaedo tells him that Socrates was
so jovial and amiable that he and the rest of Socrates'
friends did not know how to behave. Was this a time for
mourning or joy? As Socrates continued to chat and joke
with them, he was finally asked how it was possible to be
so composed, as if he were practiced in his death. Socrates
replied that for a person who correctly undertakes the
discipline of philosophy, every day is a study in dying. A
true philosopher practices death all the time, but nobody
notices it or knows in what sense he wants to die or what
kind of death it is.

Socrates' argument was that a person should understand that death is no more than a separation of the soul from the body and that a wise man tries to do this very thing his whole life long, for the body is a great hindrance in his search for Truth. It requires constant maintenance, food and sleep. It is prey to a host of ailments and diseases, and worst of all, even when, in his leisure, one may speculate on the nature of things, the mind confounds the process by generating all manner of desire, fears, fantasies and endless nonsense and rubbish. The soul while ensnared in the body and confused by the senses, reels like a drunkard, unable to grasp the essence of things, the pure archetypal realities which alone are of supreme worth.

It is a universal law that what is pure cannot be understood by what is impure, so a philosopher's first duty in life is purification. Purification is nothing more than the separation of the soul from the body. Each sense-impression is like a spike that nails the soul to the body and contaminates the sage's inquiry. In life, he comes closest to Truth when he is furthest removed from the body. So for a man who seeks the Truth, whose whole life has been a rehearsal of death, a striving for this purifying separation, to waiver when death actually comes would be ridiculous. Socrates said that if you witness a man cowering and fretting at the hour of death, that man is no lover of wisdom, he is a lover of the body.

The wise man, however, has no fear of loss because he has no love for the body. While living a sage accustoms his soul to separate from the body and to collect itself outside it and dwell free from the confines of its prison-house. At death, many pretend to make this journey, but few are able to, and these are those who have properly loved wisdom. Socrates said that every effort of his life had been towards becoming one of these few and that according to his ability he had left nothing undone. As the ´swans, when they are about to die, in anticipation of the existence to follow, sing more gloriously than ever before, so he, a brother to the swans,[3] would welcome his death.

When questioned about the soul's state after death, Socrates told his companions that people who think that death will cancel out all their misdeeds are much deluded. The soul, being immortal, needs constant care throughout many lives. There is no escape from the consequences of one's actions save through wisdom and purification. Indeed, particularly polluted souls who fear and hate and avoid the Truth that a philosopher seeks are again and again dragged down to an earthly existence. The purified soul, however, goes to the realm of the immortal gods and resides there eternally—pure, free and joyful.

Because the West has lost touch with its own traditions, such thoughts may appear to be "Eastern" on the surface. Yet Socrates was not unique in his espousal of the philosophy that the soul resides in many bodies in the course of its long struggle toward perfection. Even before his time, Pythagoras, sometimes regarded as founder of Western philosophy, saw, like the ancient Indian rishis, that the universe was always in a state of flux and followed the principles of cause and effect or *karma*. No one who reads his words as quoted by Ovid can fail to be moved by Pythagoras' eloquent speech and his belief in the immortality of the soul.

> Since I have set sail upon a wide ocean and spread my canvas to the wind, let me continue further. Nothing

is constant in the whole world. Everything is in a state of flux and comes into being as a transient appearance. Time itself flows on with constant motion, just like a river: for no more than a river can the fleeting hour stand still. As wave is driven on by wave and, itself pursued, pursues the one before, so the moments of time at once flee and follow and are ever new. What was before is left behind; that which was not comes to be, and every minute gives place to another. You see the nights, completed, pass into day; the shining rays of morning succeed the darkness of the night.

Or again, don't you see the year passing through a succession of four seasons, thus imitating our own life? In the early spring, it is tender and full of sap, like the age of childhood. Then the crops in spring trim but still delicate shoot up in the fields and though they are not yet stout and strong, fill the farmers with joyous hopes. Everything is in flower; the fertile earth, gay with brightly colored blossoms, but there is as yet no sturdiness in the leaves. Spring past, the year grows more robust and moving on into summer, becomes like a strong young man. There is no time hardier than this, none richer, none so hot and fiery. Autumn takes over when the ardour of youth is gone, a season ripe and mellow, in temper midway between youth and age, with a sprinkling of grey hairs at its temples. Then aged winter comes shivering in, with tottering steps, its hair all gone, or what it has turned white.

In the same way, our own bodies are always ceaselessly changing, and what we have been, or now are, we shall not be tomorrow. There was a day when we lived in our mother's womb, mere seeds that held the first promise of a man. To these nature applied her hands, skillfully fashioning them. Then, unwilling that our bodies should lie tightly cramped and buried inside our mother's swollen shape, she sent us out from our home into the empty air. The baby, first born into the light of day, lies weak and helpless; after that he crawls on all fours, moving his limbs as

animals do, and gradually on legs as yet trembling
and unsteady stands upright, supporting himself by
some convenient prop. Then he becomes strong and
swift of foot, passing through the stage of youth
until having lived through the years of middle age
also, he slips down the incline of old age, towards
life's setting. Age undermines and destroys the
strength of former years. Milon, grown old, weeps to
see those arms hanging limp and thin, whose massive
knotted muscles once rivalled those of Hercules.
Helen weeps too, when she sees herself in the glass,
wrinkled with age, and asks herself why she was twice
carried off. Time, the devourer, and the jealous
years that pass destroy all things and nibbling them
away, consume them gradually in a lingering death.

Nor does anything retain its own appearance perma-
nently. Ever-inventive nature continually produces
one shape after another. Nothing in the entire universe ever perishes, believe me, but the things vary,
and adopt a new form. The phrase "being born" is
used for beginning to be something different from
what one was before, while "dying" means ceasing
to be the same. Though this thing may pass into
that, and that into this, yet the sum of things remains
unchanged.

To conclude Pythagoras' remarks we return to the
beginning of his speech, as follows:

I joy to journey among the stars, high above, to leave
the earth and this dull abode, to ride from afar on
men as they wander aimlessly, devoid of any guiding
principle, to unroll for them the scroll of fate, and
cheer their panic and their fear of death, saying:
'You people, dismayed by the fear of icy death, why
are you terrified by the Styx, by shadows and empty
names, the stuff of poet's tales, by the dangers of a
world that does not exist? Our bodies, whether
destroyed by the flames of the funeral pyre, or by
slow decay, do not feel any suffering—you must not
think so. Our souls are immortal, and are ever received into new homes, where they live and dwell,
when they have left their previous abode. I myself

at the time of the Trojan war—for I remember it
well—was Panthous' son, Euphorbus, who once
received full in the breast the heavy spear of Mene-
alaus, Atreus' younger son. Quite recently, in the
temple of Juno at Argos, Abas' city, I recognized the
shield I used to carry on my left arm. All things
change, but nothing dies: the spirit wanders hither
and thither, taking possession of what limbs its
pleases, passing from beasts into human bodies, or
again our human spirit passes into beasts, but never
at any time does it perish. Like pliant wax which,
stamped with new designs, does not remain as it was,
or keep the same shape, but yet is still itself, so I
tell you that the soul is always the same, but in-
corporates itself in different forms. Therefore, in
case family feeling prove less strong than greedy
appetite, I warn you, do not drive souls that are
akin to yours out of their homes by impious kill-
ings, do not nourish blood with blood.[4]

Socrates' conduct at his death was in the finest
tradition of classical Greece and grew out of the very
philosophy he espoused and lived. As he awaited his own
execution, Socrates advised his students that every wise
person keeps the eminence of death ever in the fore-
ground of his mind, and like an incantation he continually
reminds himself of the soul's precarious residence in an
ephemeral body.

We read in *Phaedo* of Socrates' interactions with his
disciples just before his death:

When he had done speaking, Crito, one of his disciples said, "And have you any commands for us,
Socrates; anything to say about your children or any
other matter in which we can serve you?"
"Nothing particular, Crito," he replied.
"Only as I have always told you, take care of yourself. That is a service which you may be ever render-
ing to me and mine and to all of us, whether you
promise to do so or not. But if you have no thought

for yourself and care not to walk according to the
rule which I have prescribed for you, not now for the
first time, however much you may profess or promise
at the moment it will be of no avail."

"We will do our best," said Crito. "And in what way
shall we bury you?"

"Oh, in any way that you like, but you must get
hold of me and take care that I do not run away from
you!"

Then he turned to us and added with a smile, "I
cannot make Crito believe that I am the same Socrates that has been talking and conducting the argument. He fancies that I am the other Socrates whom
he will soon see a dead boy, and he asks how shall
he bury me; and though I have spoken many words
in the endeavor to show that when I have drunk the
poison, I shall leave you and go to the joys of the
blessed, these words of mine with which I was com-
forting you and myself have had, as I perceive, no
effect on Crito, and therefore I want you to be surety
for me to him now, as at the trial he was surety to the
judges for me. Let the promise be of another sort, for
he was surety for me to the judges that I would remain, and you must be my surety to him that I shall
not remain but go away and depart, and then he will
suffer less at my death and not be grieved when he
sees my body being burned or buried. I would not
have him sorrow at my hard lot or say at the burial,
'Thus really is Socrates, or thus we follow him to the
grave or bury him' for false words which are not
only evil in themselves but they infect the soul with
evil. Be of good cheer then, Crito, and say that you
are burying my body only and do with that whatever is yours and what you think best."

Now the hour of sunset was near, for a good deal of
time had passed while he was within. When he came
out, he sat down with us again after his bath but
not much was said. Soon the jailer entered and stood
by him saying,

"To you, Socrates, whom I know to be the noblest
and gentlest and best of all who ever came to this
place, I would not impute the angry feelings of other

men who rage and swear at me when in obedience to the authorities I bid them drink the poison. Indeed, I am sure that you will not be angry with me for others, as you are aware, and not I, are to blame. So fare you well and try to bear lightly what must needs be. You know my rent." Then bursting into tears the jailer turned away and went out. Socrates looked at him and said,

"I return you good wishes and will do as you bid." Then, turning to us he said, "How charming the man is. Since I have been in prison he has always been coming to see me, and at times he would talk to me and was as good to me as could be. Now see how generously he sorrows on my account. We must do as he says, Crito, and therefore let the cup be brought, if the poison is prepared; if not, let the attendant prepare some."

"Yes, " said Crito. "The sun is still upon the hilltops, and I know that many a one has taken the draught late, and after the announcement has been made to him he has eaten and drunk and enjoyed the society of his friends. Do not hurry; there is time enough."

Socrates said, "Yes, Crito, and they of whom you speak are right in so acting for they think that they will be gainers by the delay, but I am right in not following their example. For I do not think that I should gain anything by drinking the poison a little later. I should only be ridiculous in my own eyes for sparing and saving a life which is forfeit. Please, then, do as I say and not refuse me."

Crito made a sign to the servant who was standing by, and he went out and having been absent for some time, returned with the jailer, carrying the cup of poison. Socrates said, "You, my good friend, who are experienced in these matters shall give me directions how I am to proceed."

The man said, "You have only to walk about until your legs are heavy and then to lie down and the poison will act. At the same time, he handed the cup to Socrates who in the easiest and gentlest manner, without the least fear or change of color or feature, looking at the man with all his eyes, took the cup and

said, "What do you say about making a libation out of this cup to any God?" (It was customary in the ancient civilizations never to partake of anything without first making it an offering). "May I or not?" The jailer said, "Well, we only prepare, Socrates, just so much as we deem enough for one person."
"I understand," he said, "but I may and must ask the Gods to prosper my journey from this to the other world even so. And so be it according to my prayer."

Then raising the cup to his lips, quite readily and cheerfully he drank of the poison, and hitherto most of us had been able to control our sorrow, but now when we saw him drinking and saw that he had finished the draught we could no longer forebear and in spite of myself my own tears were flowing fast so that I covered my face and wept, not for him but at the thought of my own calamity and having to part from such a friend. Nor was I the first, for Crito, when he found himself unable to restrain his tears, had got up, and I followed, and at that moment Apollodorus, who had been weeping all the time, broke in a loud and passionate cry which made cowards of us all. Socrates alone retained his calmness.
"What is this strange outcry," he said. "I sent away the women mainly in order that they might not misbehave in this way, for I have been told that a man should die in peace. Be quiet then and have patience."

When we heard his words we were ashamed and refrained our tears, and he walked about until, as he said, his legs began to fail, and then he lay on his back according to the directions, and the man who gave him the poison, now and then looked at his feet and legs, and after a while he pressed his foot hard and asked if he could feel and he said no; then his leg and so upwards and showed us that he was cold and stiff, and he felt them himself and said that when the poison reaches the heart, that will be the end. He was beginning to grow cold about the groin when he uncovered his face for he had covered himself up, and said, "Crito, I owe a cock to Esclepius. Will you

> remember to pay the debt?"
> "The debt will be paid," said Crito. "Is there any-
> thing else?"
> There was no answer to this question, but in a minute
> or two a movement was heard, and the attendants
> uncovered him; his eyes were set and Crito closed
> his eyes and mouth. Such was the end of our friend
> concerning whom I may truly say that of all the men
> of his time whom I have known he was the wisest
> and justest and the best."[5]

This account only lends support to the truth that
great men teach not only through their lives but more so
through the manner of their death. Even though the
contemporary Western philosophers "in general . . . wish
to exclude the subject of death from the area of legiti-
mate philosophical speculation[6] the Gnostics believed in
the ever-pure nature of the Self, to which the body is a
mere material encumbrance. The Stoics agreed with the
Yoga attitude that

> to overcome the fear of death, we must think of it
> constantly . . . in the proper manner . . . The fear of
> death displays a baseness wholly incompatible with
> the dignity and calm of the true philosopher who has
> learned to emancipate himself from finite concerns
> . . . The Stoic outlook was the Platonic view that
> philosophizing means learning to die.[7]

Leonardo da Vinci may have read of Solon when he
said, "Just as a day well spent brings happy sleep, so . . . a
life well spent brings happy death."[8] This view was held
not only by the ancient and medieval philosophers but,
"It also appears to be the view of most pragmatists and of
Bertrand Russell."[9]

Schopenhauer is known as one of the most influ-
ential in the history of the modern philosophy of Europe.
He attributed the origins of his philosophy to the

Upanishads, the Sanskrit texts that have recorded the dialogues between ancient masters and disciples dating 2,000-600 B.C. Schopenhauer believed that one should,

> . . . achieve a state of indifference or pure will-less-ness—a state best known in moments of pure aesthetic contemplation but to which the awareness of death substantially contributes.

> According to Nietzche, the superior man will not permit death to seek him out in ambush, to strike him down unaware. The superior man will live constantly in the awareness of death, joyfully and proudly . . .

> Heidegger and Sartre, like most existentialists, urge us to cultivate the awareness of death chiefly as a means of heightening our sense of life . . .

> Heidegger makes the additional claim . . . that the awareness of death confers upon man a sense of his own individuality . . . To shut out the conscious-ness of death is, therefore, to refuse one's individual-ity and to live inauthentically.[10]

These are exactly the attitudes in India. All these Western philosophers have been studied by scholars to compare their thought in other areas with that of India, but not yet on the subject of death.

It was Wordsworth who recognized the presence of divine spirit in the mind of man, as does the yoga tradition in order to search for God within:

> For I have learned
> To look on nature, not as in the hour
> Of thoughtless youth; but hearing often time
> The still, sad music of humanity,
> Not harsh nor grating, though of ample power
> To chasten and subdue. And I have felt
> A presence that disturbs me with the joy
> Of elevated thoughts; a sense sublime

Of something far more deeply interfused,
Whose dwelling is the light of setting suns,
And the round ocean and the living air,
And the blue sky, and in the mind of man:
A motion and a spirit, that impels
All thinking things, all objects of all thought,
And rolls through all things.

So, to him, death and rebirth are linked:

Our birth is but a sleep and a forgetting
The soul that rises with us, our life's star
Hath had elsewhere its setting,
And cometh from afar.
Not in entire forgetfulness
And not in utter nakedness
But trailing clouds of glory do we come
From God who is our home.
Heaven lies about us in our infancy;
Shades of the prison house begin to close
Upon the growing boy;
But he beholds the light, and whence it flows
He sees it in his joy.
The youth who daily farther from the East
Must travel, still is nature's priest,
And by the vision splendid
Is on his way attended.
At length the man perceives it die away
And fade into the light of common day.

An article in the weekly London periodical, *The Spectator*, stated: "There did not seem, until recently, to be any definite reference to the belief (of reincarnation) in Wordsworth's poems for well known lines, 'Our birth is but a sleep and a forgetting' are a statement of the soul's pre-existence, rather than of its repeated returns to earth. But the newly discovered poem in (his sister) Dorothy Wordsworth's handwriting provides remarkable evidence of the poet's interest in this age-old doctrine. The lines are addressed to an infant, and begin as follows:

Oh, sweet new-comer to the changeful earth,

If, as some darkling seers have boldly guessed,
Thou hadst a being and a human birth,
And wert erewhile by human parents blessed,
Long, long before thy present mother pressed
Thee, helpless stranger, to her fostering breast . . .[11]

Shelley, the romantic poet, while taking a walk with a friend in the park was talking about death and previous existence. Being a man of very spontaneous action he saw a woman coming across the lawn with a baby in her arms and went over and grabbed the child from the astonished mother, who for a moment thought that he was kidnapping her baby! Instead, however, he asked to question the child about pre-existence and to tell them from where he had come. The woman replied that the child could not speak yet. Shelley said that that was probably only a whim as only a year or two ago he was speaking and could not have forgotten how to so early.[12]

One of the greatest philosophers the West has ever produced was Emanuel Kant. The philosophy of Kant has been compared with the philosophy of Shankara of India. Kant's influence was felt all the way down through the generations of philosophers in Europe and up to the transcendentalist writers of the United States, Emerson and Thoreau.

Generation in the human race depends
on many accidents, on occasion on the
views and whims of government, nay even on vice,
so that it is difficult to believe in the
external existence of a being whose life has
first begun under certain circumstances so
trivial and so entirely dependent on our own
choice it would seem as if you could hardly expect so
wonderful an effect from causes so insignificant.
But, in answer to these objections we may adduce
the transcendental hypothesis that all life

> is improperly intelligible and not subject
> to the changes of time and that it neither
> began in birth nor will end in death.
>
> If we could see ourselves and other
> objects as they really are, we should see
> ourselves in a world of spiritual natures,
> our community with which neither began at
> our birth nor will end with the death of
> the body.[13]

The mortality of the body, its destiny to dust (Gen. 3:10; Eccl. 3:19-21; Heb. 9:27; Jas. 2:26) and the physical death, the separation of the inner man from the outer man, of the soul from the body is well known to the Judaic as well as the Christian tradition.

The wise men of the Upanishads pray, "Deliver me from mortality to immortality," *"Mrtyor ma amrtam gamaya."* The Catholic priests pray on the Day of All Souls: "Deliver me, Lord, from eternal death," *"Liberate me, Domine, de morte aeterna."*

As the ancient Vedic rishi prayed for *Amrtam Jyotih*: the immortal light, so does the Western priest of today beseech God: *"Lux aeterna luceat:* may the eternal light shine."

To the Vedic rishi, God is the one, *yasya chaya amrtam*, under whose shade is immortality. And the Christian priest says: *Justorum animae in manu dei sunt*, the souls of the just are in the hand of God. In Atharvaveda, we are assured: *na marishyasi, na marishyasi, ma bibheh:* thou shalt not die; thou shalt not die; fear not. So in the Catholic commemoration of the saints: *visi sunt oculis insipientum mori, illi autem sunt in pace,* in the eyes of the foolish they seemed to die, but they are in peace. In St. Paul's epistle to the Corinthians (1 Cor. 15,

51-57), we read, "O death, where is thy victory? O death, where is thy sting?" And we hear in Sanskrit songs, "We have made friends with God, what can death now do to us?" *"Kim no mrtyuh karishyati."*

In spite of the fact that death is present as the "dark valley" in the Biblical thought, the deaths of great saints and martyrs of the West exhibit an exemplary mastery over the flesh. St. Francis of Assisi welcomed "sister death" with a smile. To St. Julian of Norwich Christ's death and love were one. She saw the vision of the Lord in a night of great sickness and expressed the joy of the wine of life in the evening cup of death. Speaking of Christ's death she said:

> If that I might suffer more, I would suffer more. I saw in truth that as often as He might die, so often He would, and love should never let Him have rest till He had done it. And I beheld with great diligence for to learn how often He would die if He might. And verily the number passed mine understanding and my wits so far that my reason might not, nor could, comprehend it. And when He had thus oft died, or should, yet He would set it at nought, for love; for all seemeth Him but little in regard of His love." (Revelations of Divine Love, the ninth revelation, chapter XXII, p. 47-48).

This view of death gives her the universal vision of Self, akin to yoga, when she burst out: "It is I. It is I. It is I; that is all."

As we have seen, the statements of the many other Western philosophers are identical to the teachings of the yoga texts. What is missing in the West is a living tradition of training for the conscious process of dying which is known to the yoga meditative lineage alone.

It is probable that the art of dying was at one time

taught in the West. In the *Encyclopedia Cattolica* published from the Vatican, one finds an entry under *Ars
Moriendi* (Art of Dying). There are several texts under
similar titles, published since 1465. *Ars bene moriendi*, the
art of dying correctly, is integrated with *ars bene vivendi*,
the art of living properly. Unfortunately, these texts are
extremely brief admonitions to the dying to confess, to
fear hell and die happy with faith in Christ and so forth,
but there is not a single line indicating any knowledge of
the methods for artfully separating the soul from the body.
Those interested in further investigation may write to this
author for a bibliography of references.[14]

We have made these brief references to Western
thinking only where it agrees with the yoga view. How
much of this thought was directly learned from the East
is difficult to ascertain historically, until we come to the
later Western philosophers such as Schopenhauer in
Europe and the Transcendentalist founders of American
literature such as Emerson, Thoreau and Whitman. Emerson's poem titled *Brahma* is a paraphrase from passages in
the Vishnupurana, Bhagavad Gita and the Upanishads. It
sings of the universal spirit as eternal, unborn, undying:

> If the red slayer thinks he slays,
> Or if the slain thinks he is slain,
> They know not well the subtle ways
> I keep, and pass, and turn again.
>
> Far or forgot to me is near;
> Shadow and sunlight are the same;
> The vanished gods to me appear;
> And one to me are shame and fame.
>
> They reckon ill who leave me out;
> When me they fly, I am the wings;

I am the doubter and the doubt,
And I the hymn the Brahmin sings.

The strong gods pine for my abode,
And pine in vain the sacred Seven;
But thou, meek lover of the good!
Find me, and turn thy back on heaven.

NOTES
CHAPTER 1

1. *The Histories of Herodotus*; Tr. Aubrey de Selincourt, Penguin Classics.

2. *Xenophon's Memoirs of Socrates*, Tr. Hugh Tredennick, Penguin Classics.

3. In yoga the pranas are termed swans, *hamsa* or *hamso* as in the *soham* mantra. The mystical meaning of the swan-song is the harmonious song of pranas at the hour of death. A liberated Master is referred to as *paramahamsa*, the supreme Swan, for his swan-like purity, free-winged whiteness of purity. The swans are servants of Apollo, the sun-god; in yoga also the sun is called a *hamsa*, the heavenly swan. This, because in the secretmost solar science path of yoga, the pranas flow towards and through the solar gate in the thousand-petaled lotus.

4. Summarized here from the *Metamorphoses of Ovid*, Chapter 15, Tr. May M. Innes, Penguin Classics.

5. This entire statement of Socrates is summarized here from Plato's *Phaedo*, Tr. B. Jowett; classics Club.

6. *The Encyclopedia of Philosophy*, ed. Paul Edwards, MacMillan Publishing Co., Vol. I, p. 207.

7. *Ibid.*, p. 308.

8. *Ibid.*

9. *Ibid.*

10. *Ibid.*

11. For these references, I am indebted to Mead, Joseph and Cranston, S.L., *Reincarnation: An East-West Anthology*, a Quest Book, 1975.

12. *Ibid.*

13. *Ibid.*

14. I am grateful to my friend, Rev. Father Leo Tibesar of St. Paul Seminary Library in St. Paul, Minneosta, for supplying me with these references. For further information on *Ars Moriendi*, see Evans-Wentz's introduction to his translation of the Tibetan Book of the Dead.

Birth and Death: Cycles

Alexander of Macedonia, whom some people call Great because he conquered and pillaged so much, invaded India but could not go very far into the country. According to Plutarch he searched out the wise gymno sophists in India who must have changed his mind. It is said that when he returned to Babylonia to die of his wounds he had one last wish. He said, "When I die, cover my whole body but leave my hands out of the shroud, with my palms open. Let the whole world see that out of all my conquests this is all I am taking with me!"

We are reminded of the story of Bhoja, an eighth century king. His father died leaving him under the guardianship of his own brother Munja who was appointed a regent until his nephew, the rightful heir, grew to maturity. Munja, however, coveted the kingdom for himself and ordered a minister to take the young heir to a secluded forest and slay him there. "Before I am slain by your sword, minister, do grant me a last wish. Please take a letter from me to my uncle.'' The young prince broke a leaf from a tree, borrowed the minister's sword to draw some blood. He used the blood for ink on the leaf and with a fine twig for a pen he wrote:

> King Mandhata the jewel of the golden ages is no
>   more;
> He who bridged the ocean, King Rama of the Treta
>   (the second age), too, is gone;
> Many emperors, even the likes of Yudhishthira, all
>   had to depart;
> This earth did not go with a single one of them;
> But with you it will certainly go, king!

When he saw the note, Uncle Munja swooned with grief over what he had done. Upon which the wise minister who had hidden the prince and shown to Junja a goat's eyes as proof of the murder, now produced the young boy. Bhoja grew to be one of the greatest patrons of art and learning in the history of India. The thought of death, it is proved, can be a very positive factor, in improving our moral standard and to disincline us from evil. Did not Benjamin Franklin prepare his own epitaph which someone has called the most famous of American epitaphs:

> The body of Benjamin Franklin, printer, like the cover of an old book, its contents torn out and stripped of its lettering and gilding, lies here, food for worms, but the work shall not be lost. For it will appear once more in a new and more elegant edition, revived and corrected by the author.

Death can be humorous, joyful, happy, a change. A parting of a curtain. A transition. A new approach. A new life, a new beginning. Culmination, ascendence, apex, end, completeness, perfection. Perfection is transcendence.

In order for us to understand birth it is also necessary for us to understand death, for whatever our origins are, we return to it. Idries Shah quotes Hasan of Basra:

> I saw a child carrying a light.
> I asked him where he had brought it from.
> He put it out, and said:
> "Now you tell me where it is gone."

The very thought that is born goes into the universal unconscious at the hour of death and re-emerges again at the next birth.

> The Transcendental Mother of the universe
> within whose womb these cycles go on
> is She, the Unborn, who becomes within time
> the Great Death as well as the Creation.
> —Devi Mahatmya 12.39

Our personal cycles of life and death of the body are a part of these cosmic cycles. The link between the cosmic and the personal cycles is through the subtle body which is the repository of the cosmic forces within us. These forces in the subtle body are affected through our karma as the same subtle body is also the repository of all our samskaras, the sum total of the impressions of our thoughts, actions and experiences, however subliminal.

The rhythms of the cosmic forces, when acted upon by our karmic dimensions, produce our diseases, determine our mode and moment of death, and direct us to the next incarnation. They also warn us of impending death by producing varying types of symptoms. The most ancient medical text of the world, *Charaka-Samhita*, devotes chapters 5-11 of Section Five on the prognosis of death through fantasy, dreams and physiological signs, showing in the last chapter the signs of natural imbalances which cause the medicines to be ineffective in the body. *Shiva-svarodaya*, one of the major texts on the science of breath rhythms called *svara*, devotes verses 321-369 to describing the symptoms that indicate death impending within a period of one year to immediate future. Similarly, H. H. Swami Rama has listed in *Life Here and Hereafter* thirteen signs of imminent death.

We summarize below the verses from Markandeya-Purana and Skanda-Purana quoted by Narayana Tirtha in his commentary on the yoga sutras, chapter 3, sutra 22.

> If only the left or only the right nostril is active for many days;
> if both nostrils are equally active for ten days;
> if one seems unable to see his own tongue, tip of the nose and the eyebrow center;
> if the colors are seen reversed; e.g., red for green;
> if one tastes the opposite of what is actual; e.g., bitter for sweet;
> if the throat, lips, tongue and the palate remain continuously dry;
> if the hands, feet and the cardiac area dry up even immediately after a bath;
> if one does not see his own shadow, trembles even if he is tied up to be completely still;
> the eyes, fingers and the semen begin to turn blue;
> incontinence in the matter of elimination, urination and ejaculation is consistent;
> one sees snake-like apparitions in the sky;
> the intellectual processes become confused;
> one articulates different from what he intends;
> he sees rainbows where there are none, or sees many of them in all directions;
> he sees two moons or two suns;
> he sees the moon and the stars in the day;
> sees no stars at night;
> sees the sun or the moon but no rays thereof;
> sees fantastic cities and castles on trees, plants and hilltops;
> sees ghosts dancing in the day time;
> sees the vision of a black and yellow god of death;
> sees himself being devoured by different creatures;
> a fat person suddenly becomes lean or vice-versa;
> experiences everything as opposite to its nature;

sees his reflection minus his head;
remains hungry even after a very full meal;
cannot smell the candle immediately upon blowing
  it out;
cannot see his reflection in the pupils of others'
  eyes;
cannot hear the inner sound upon closing the ears
  with the fingers;
if one's character undergoes sudden and complete
  change, e.g., a gentle person becomes violent or
  vice-versa.

There are many verses describing dreams that may be indicative of a short lifespan or impending death. A series of texts deals with the phenomenon of *chaya-purusha*, the gigantic shadow figure one sees against the clear sky after gazing at one's own shadow in the sunlight or the moonlight. Various signs in the shadowman of the sky can indicate impending death or a short remaining lifespan.

The psychic factors behind these experiences and phenomena are fully understood only by the yogis, with reference to the factors in the subtle body, the five sheaths of personality and their mutual interactions. It is the mastery over these that leads to conquest over death. Without karmic purification such conquest is impossible, and rebirth occurs as follows.

Two thought-units, the mother thought and the father thought, unite. So a tiny new thought is created. These two thoughts, the mother thought and the father thought, carry in their wake the total essences of the bodies in which they previously dwelt. The essences of the mother-body and the father-body, helpless in the wake of the two thoughts uniting, merge. Thereby a new body for the fresh new thought resulting from the union of the mother thought and the father thought is brought into composition, comes into being. This thought at the moment is germinal, barely aware of its own being. The essences of the mother body and the father body have joined together to house this tiny thought and the new body, a microscopic being, clings to the wall of the mother's uterus. The thought grows. Little flashes begin to occur as the thought grows. The body grows in its wake. The mind, like an octopus, hangs out its extensions along the edges of the extensions of that body. Little limbs begin to develop and soon the creature is ready to leave the first house that it occupied—the mother's womb. At that time the articulate thought "I am" is not present; only the non-verbal feel "I am" is present. Only the non-verbal thought is present. The thought grows, grows on the diet of other thoughts that are introduced. The thought of the food being placed in the mouth makes the thought possessive. The thought that the body is eliminating something from the nether end, from the lower centers of consciousness, gives the ability to reject things and people. The thought grows and learns that this body can be made to walk. The body walks; the body speaks. This being grows together with the thought and the body becomes a youthful one, is attracted to the opposite sex, marries, reproduces further thoughts, becomes the mother thought or the father thought for further thoughts to grow and gives them bodies from the quintessence of its own body. The body gets sick, the thought recognizes that fact. The body gets old; the thought recognizes that fact, too. The body lies in the position of a corpse but the thought which still is alive, also recognizes this fact.

So does a person fall asleep, and before he begins to fall asleep his mind is whirling around with the matters of the world; slowly the mind begins to settle down; a negation begins to overtake him and soon he is aware, barely aware, only of the walls of the room. He withdraws further; soon he is aware only of the bed and the blankets. If you watch yourself falling asleep you will see that you are passing through these processes; you are now aware mainly of the extremities of your body—hands and feet and the surfaces. Gradually the consciousness withdraws and withdraws and becomes aware only of the centers of consciousness, from the navel to the brain. And then you withdraw upwards and soon you are aware only of the mind, only of the world in the mind. All kinds of thoughts and fancies and fantasies appear which then again settle down, are negated, and the person is fast asleep . . . which is the perfect model of death, or of meditation.

When we wake up the first thought we are aware of is: I am. The aware "I am" becomes aware of the skull where the thought is, becomes aware of the eyes from where the thought looks out into the world, becomes aware of the other centers of consciousness: the throat as the speech center, the heart as the emotion center, the navel center, the genital center, the elimination centers. Slowly the conscious thought extends itself and recognizes that it has these twiddling toes and wiggling fingers, becomes aware of the covers. For a moment he doesn't even know whether he is sleeping with his head east, north, south or west. Where am I? How did I turn around this way? Am I in a motel or in my house? Slowly, the orientation returns. The thought becomes aware of the room, then the whole world. This is the paradigm of the cycle of birth and death.

A child is born—as he grows, from the age of zero to the age of five years and nine months, including the nine months that he dwells in the uterus, he slowly becomes aware of himself. Very little is he aware of the things around him. Slowly he knows that something, the breast, comes closer and fills him and fulfills him. Gradually he knows that somebody pinches; somebody touches him. A feeling in the extremities of the body begins. He becomes aware of a room, becomes aware of a house, becomes aware of a family. Goes to sleep after a day of seventy or eighty solar years[1] and now here he lies! The thought is again ready to fold its own blanket upon itself. He knows all his family members who have loved him.

He thinks "Have I loved them, have I cared for them, have I not cared for them?" There is satisfaction, contentment, peace if I have done everything that I ought to have done. there is contentment, satisfaction, warmth, joy if they have loved me, if they have cared for me. Yes, they are all here, the extensions of my body, the extensions of my thought; the thought germs I have planted in other bodies, my son, my daughters, my fellow thought cousins, my brothers, my sisters; the thoughts from whom I was born; the thought from whom I, this present thought, was made; my parents, grandparents. I, who am in mind, who am part of a greater mind, in whom all of these thought whirlpools in my surrounding arise, this particular complex of thought bubbles is all happy with me. I am happy with them. I have a feeling of warmth, joy; a little tear comes. Sorry to be going, but it has been good, and thank you all!

If we have completed our karmic duties and paid our karmic debts in this life, if we have been loved and cared for, if we have not been left to die alone in some nursing home, then a mental farewell is said. Gradually the dying person mentally withdraws. If there has been love, and the resultant contentment, he withdraws more easily. One is secure. There isn't the grabbing, a clutching for things which have left one dissatisfied, incomplete. "Oh, I'd like to do this. Oh, I'd like to complete that. Oh, I never got that done. Oh, my son never cared for me. Maybe even now, there is something, something that can happen, whereby he can love me. Let me try to keep my eyes open; let me not die; let me not go away. The thought I've created so fondly, maybe that thought knows its union with me, will join me, will love me?" So the conflict remains if the duties have not been done on both sides.

At first the dying person has all these memories, all the things about which he has conflicts, all the things that he has yet left incomplete. He denies to himself that he is dying, he thinks that he is going to get up and complete all of those things; that he is going to settle many matters yet, that he is going to pay all his debts, that the love he has not received in life he will yet receive. Anyway, slowly he comes face to face with the fact of death. He withdraws, and is aware not of the world but barely of the walls of the room around him. How much he is aware of the relatives, friends, loved ones around him is uncertain. He is very much aware of their presence in the mind; I'm not saying that he's aware in the mind of their presence, but he's aware of their presence in the mind, the memories, the fact of their having been. And gradually a stage arrives where the world within him and the world without lose their distinct boundary lines.

Dissatisfaction remains; it tears the mind apart. It pulls the dying apart. The dying one who has to go, does not want to go. By loving them today, we let them die in peace fifty years from now. Let us do something in life that would let everyone die in peace, even though we are not thinking of their death now. There is or there is not conflict at the hour of death, depending on the kind of life we have lived, the kind of karmic fulfillments we have brought in life to ourselves and to others, especially to others; the kind of love we have received or have given.

There are five stages through which a dying person passes says Kubler-Ross. First of these is denial. People deny to themselves the fact of death; they even deny to themselves the fact of being sick—just as alcoholics deny to themselves that they are alcoholics. The persons suffering from cancer deny to themselves that they have a terminal disease. Why do they pass through this kind of denial? Because there is a part of themselves that wishes to complete something that was left incomplete. They need to fulfill something that has not yet been fulfilled. Therefore the degree of conflict, of self-denial, of depression, the degree of tearing of the flesh from the soul at the hour of death depends on the kind of life lived and on the way our relationships have developed.

Willingly or unwillingly, with contentment or with resentment, an insomniac falls asleep. One dies in the same manner. Not being able to sleep easily is a disease. Not being able to die easily is also a disease. Dying is no disease; only not being able to die is the disease. Hanging on there, not wanting to go, clutching the external awareness, not wanting to sleep, a hidden part of the person keeping him awake when he should be asleep, keeping him here when he should be gone—we must recognize this disease of not being able to die happily. In India, to bring about a change of mood, the dying person is reminded to bring his thoughts to God. All discussion of worldly matters should cease in his presence. He should not hear the sound of anyone crying lest his mind and soul be distracted, the trauma be further compounded, and attachment to body, to its surroundings and to its relationships with the kin delay his departure. All emotional disturbances caused at such a time will disturb the subtle body, prevent a smooth departure. The soul will have no peace. Special mantras are uttered into his right ear. Other recitations and chants and scriptural passages are recited in his presence. He is advised to focus his mind on silently repeating a name of God or a mantra.

At the hour of death, all kinds of memories of the past and projections of the future, merge with the present reality. One is lying in the hospital room, but thinks he is lying in a holy temple in India; these could be memories of the past, unfulfilled longings, wishes for the future, or projections of where he might be going. Many dimensions of spaces and times, many sequences and causations overlap because the whirl of thought is folding back upon itself and is using parts of its own self as blankets to cover itself up.

Let us look further into these very cycles. A child is born and throws his hands and feet all over. A person is dying, throws his hands and feet all over. There seems to be no direction to his reflexes, they are not under his control. We need to understand here the connections between the consciousness and the body. The consciousness which is linked to the fine instrument of *buddhi*, the instrument of intelligence and discrimination which is linked to the active mind, which is linked to the brain and the reflexes through the spine, through the nervous system, through the muscles and so forth. If the harmony has not been fully established the consciousness that has come into the new body is yet experimenting about the ways of adjusting itself to take control of the new castle in which it suddenly finds itself. When the consciousness becomes used to the castle, then it knows all its byways, corridors, chambers, dungeons, turrets and spires from head to toe. Then we say that the child has developed control of the neuro-muscular apparatus. A child falls asleep and we find that he goes through the same motions as a dying person goes through. He tosses and turns, protests, then after a while his consciousness withdraws from the surroundings and he settles down, barely a sensation of awareness in the hands, feet and the face remains. He continues to withdraw and is now aware only of the centers of consciousness. Slowly withdrawing again from the stomach, the heart and the throat center we are aware only of the thought center. The thought folds back upon itself, uses a part of itself as though a blanket. The last thought trails off. Before we know it we have fallen asleep. This we do every time we fall asleep.

A person goes to sleep at night. He lies in bed, is aware of the whole world, of everything he has done during the day. Slowly the consciousness begins to withdraw. It is only aware of the four walls of the room. The consciousness withdraws further, is aware only of the bed and the covers. It withdraws yet further and is aware only of the extremities of the body. The bed and the covers are forgotten. Exactly thus does a person die. For a while he is not certain what he is thinking of saying and what he is actually saying. He utters disjointed sentences and people think, "Ah, he's said something, I couldn't understand." But in his mind the sentence is complete. The way a child learns to speak, the same process is reversed. When a child says "toy," seeing it in a shop window, the entire sentence is clear in his mind, "Mother, come, buy this toy for me." His thought is completely clear. But we who are insensitive and dependent on external language, its grammatical structures and its syntactical conventions do not fully understand what he is saying. A dying person passes through the same process in reverse. Where previously when an infant was learning to speak, the speech developed from the mind, now the speech is being withdrawn into the mind.

Soon he is aware only of the extremities of his body. Gradually he withdraws further and is aware only of certain basic centers of consciousness. He withdraws inwards, the eyes turn inwards, the world of the mind becomes more real, he does not know he is dying. In most cases, in the actual process of death the idea of death vanishes. Only so long as the conscious processes of speech and language about death linger on, there remains the idea

of death. In the actual process of death itself the conscious idea and the preconceived notions about death all
vanish in the same way as you are sitting and listening to
me here but you are not saying "I am living, I am living,
I am living." You are not saying, "I am hearing, I am
hearing, I am hearing." So the person dying also at that
stage does not say, "I am dying, I am dying, I am dying,"
because he is so busy experiencing the world within.
He has no time for conforming to our conventions. Spaces
have completely curved back and the cycle is complete.
They are turning back to that very point where they
started to draw the circle from. The end is the beginning;
the beginning is the end. It is the beginning of the whole
creation. It is the time of our daily awakening in the
morning. It is the time every time we have taken birth on
this planet or any other planet. It is the time that we have
died every time.

So the body that was so beloved of the wife, the
body that was so adored of the husband—you can not stay
with it for a day. Come, hurry, put it in a nice little
casket. Put on it the best possible clothes. Let's go bury
it, cremate it, turn it to ashes. What else can you do with
this dead thing? It is of no use.

The human consciousness recognizes that the body
is nothing. That it is not the body we have loved. We
cannot have made love to the body when we were having
sex, otherwise we would have been attracted to this dead
body also. In all of us there remains a recognition that
there is a live principle. In all of us, life always recognizes
life. If a baby just born could crawl and were shown a
living face and a wooden face, the child, knowing

absolutely nothing about the theory of life and non-life, would crawl towards that which is living.

We dress up our dead bodies as if they are going to a party. That is a custom all over the world. The dress that the person liked the best is put on him. In India, before a person dies, he is asked of any special desires; not what should be done with his possessions, but what is his last wish. Generally the person may have the desire to eat something. That food would always be given to him.

Another practice that is very common in India is for a dying mother to call all her children and put one last morsel of food in each one's mouth with her own hand. In life she gave the breast to the child. At death she still performs the act of feeding.

The father calls all his children and places his hand on their heads as a gesture of blessing, as it were, passing on the life forces to them. These customs are practiced to show our final love; they are the final gestures of farewell out of closeness that is present. And because the body belongs to someone we love, we dress it up.

In modern times as soon as a doctor declares an ill person to be beyond relief, he is brought home. The dying person is brought down to lie on earth—to be in the arms of the mother earth. A wick is lit by his headside which is extinguished only after death. If he dies in the hospital he is taken immediately to his home. In India the body is not kept long. It is not possible to do so in the heat of that country where the funeral industry has not yet developed and it does not cost thousands of dollars to die.

In China, the custom used to be that upon reaching middle age a person would go out and select a tree, have the best carpenter available build a casket for him with loving hands. Or one might even build his own casket and keep it under his own bed. He would look at it fondly, and looked forward to that death which would be a union with his ancestors. This whole Confucian idea is very similar to that in India of relationship with the living elders and the departed. The thought of a debt owed towards them persists. One of the reasons why persons should have children (either their own or adopted) is because of the debt that is owed to parents for the care received when one was a child. There is no way that we can give that care to parents, but the karmic debt remains, so we pay the debt by doing for someone in an identical situation that which was done for us. This is the way of paying a karmic debt: whatever good was done for me in any situation should be done by me for someone else. My debt to my parents is paid by giving to my children what my parents gave to me.

> When one has once seen the face of one's son, the debt owed to the parents is paid off.
> —Garuda Purana, Part II, Ch. 15, v. 29

This is also one of the reasons the institution of marriage exists, for otherwise you die not having paid the karmic debt and then there are all kinds of emotional dissatisfactions in life which you do not consciously recognize as related to the unfulfilled karmas, but which are very much there.

When the people of India know that life will not continue they often go away on a long pilgrimage. They have voluntarily left behind all their connections. They have already willingly given up that which would otherwise be taken away by force. When you give something up voluntarily, then you do not suffer its loss. When it is taken from you by force, then you suffer. They have learned this art of giving up, of renouncing, of walking away and turning their backs on everything. Between the ages of 50 or 60, a person should give up the worldly affairs to their children. It does not always happen that way. People everywhere grab onto a great deal of attachments, and consequently suffer.

If in life one has been unable to fulfill the wish for a pilgrimage, then even after death the body is taken to a place of pilgrimage to fulfill that desire. Sometimes the corpse is taken many hundred miles on four shoulders to holy places to be cremated, if such had been the person's wish. One of my memories as a child is of sitting in a restaurant in the holy city of Varanasi and seeing the corpses being carried on four shoulders. They came from many hundred miles away, walking all the way. The corpse was tied on a bamboo bier, covered with a cloth.

The corpse is taken and put on a huge pile of logs. The body is covered with more logs and a lot of special type of incense powder and ghee, clarified butter, is poured with chanting of special mantras and prayers. Each organ, each component of the body is named, followed by the word *Svaha*: this is a sacred offering, carried upwards by the fire, taken to its origins.

> May your eyes mingle with the sun.
> May your breath be merged with the cosmic winds.
> May the waters of your being mingle with the oceans.
> May the ashes become one with the earth.
> May you go to the heavens or to the earth,
>   whatever your direction may be.
>   —Yajur Veda, ch. 39

Then people watch the fire as it burns. When the corpse is burned and the fire goes down, the people turn their backs, take a little piece of straw, break it behind their backs, and walk away. Or they smash a clay jar on the ground. This type of act is expressive of the thought that something is gone, broken, with nothing more to do. This is it!

Everybody's thought at that time turns to God. This is the end of life. Only one question arises: What am I going to do with my own life that remains? Everything that is preached at that time indicates an awareness that ultimately this is where we all are going. All our possessions, power, ego, all our pride of beauty and handsomeness, success and everything else—this is it; this is the end. Remember this as you stand there, cremating another corpse. Remember this is the path you will be taking. This is where you are going. Turn your mind to God.

There is a story of the great 16th century saint-poet, Kabir. Someone wanted to meet him, and had walked a long way to see him. The villagers said, "He is not here. He has gone to a funeral."

The visitor was in a rush to see Kabir, so he said, "I will go where the funeral is taking place." He questioned, "How will I know Kabir when I see him there?"

They replied, "Kabir wears a feather on his cap."

When the man went to the funeral, he saw that everybody had a feather in his cap. He was amazed. As the funeral procession dispersed, one person's feather disappeared. As another of the party went two steps, his feather disappeared. Another went four steps when his feather disappeared. So one by one each person's feather vanished at varying distances. The only one whose feather remained was the saint, Kabir. The feather is the thoughts that we all develop at the time about the unreality, the transience of our very important affairs and pursuits, of the ways we cherish our fixations, of the ways we develop our diversions, our pet dogmas, depressions, hidden angers, revenges, power and ambitions.

Here a few remarks need to be addressed to the counselor and to the therapist who have taken the position an elder or a priest has in the more traditional societies, and now carries that responsibility.

We shall later refer to the words of Rama, spoken to his brother: "As two pieces of wood come together on the waves of a river by the action of the waves and force of the winds and float along for a while, so when our karma is over, that momentum is broken and like the pieces of wood, each of us goes his way."

If you teach the right philosophy, then a terminal patient should know that there is a part of his mind which is still useful to which he can withdraw, into which he can take a dip. There is something within him to which he can turn his mind.

So, taking the question of a terminal cancer patient who sees no purpose to his life, what do you do with him? What do you advise him to do? He says, "I want to kill myself. I want the doctor to give me a shot to terminate my life." We need an answer from a meditative point of view to someone who sees no further use to his body and is losing all hope. Through one's spiritual power, one may gradually raise the level of consciousness so that even though the physical pain may increase, the mental suffering decreases.

We have to teach people to learn to separate physical pain from mental suffering. Let the same attitude develop with reference to your own problems. Contemplate this for a moment as you read: separate physical pain from the mental suffering.

Learn to separate the mental pain from physical suffering by giving something worthwhile to the mind to think about. It can be a Catholic Father or a Lutheran minister, or a Rabbi saying, "Surrender to the grace of God." It can be a scientist, who would like to make one last great discovery before dying. If people have a clear idea that they are worthwhile, that the spirit itself is undeniably free of pain, then they learn to take a dip into that area of the spirit. And though the body is wasted, there is still, up to the last minute in a human being, a part of the mind that is always clear. Like meditation, the art of a therapist is to let a person come in touch with that part of the mind and to reinforce it, so that he sees his physical pain very objectively as a witness, the way you first look at the world when you open your eyes from deep meditation, like a procession passing before you.

There is a beautiful koan in the Zen tradition. A disciple is told to stand on a bridge and watch the water flow; slowly he realizes the true meaning of the koan: the water stood still, the bridge was flowing. This, too, is the meaning of the separation of the physical pain from mental suffering. So that the terminal patient knows that for this body that he had for a little while, time has come. Even if this body stayed free of disease for a thousand years, some time, somewhere, this moment has to come.

I have used this body for awhile, and now this body is a worn out machine. It is a vehicle I have used. I cannot prevent this wood from rotting; it has taken much exposure of all kinds for years or centuries and must now retire.

The second chapter of the Bhagavad Gita is the most popular reading in India at the occasion of death because here you have this man, Arjuna, who is afraid of fighting and of dying. He is advised to go into the battlefield. He is told to pick up his weapons. The fear is strong in him. The uncertainties baffle him.

> Oh, Krishna, I cannot stand. This bow is slipping from my hands. My skin is burning, my head is going round and round. I will not fight.

He lets his bow slip and sits down on the back seat. Krishna looks at him and says:

> What are you afraid of? What are your fears? Stand up! Fight! Fight without fever. Because, O Arjuna, this body is made up of elements of matter. It is composed so it has to decompose. Anything that at some time was not at some other time shall definitely cease to be. There was a time when this body was not, so the time has to come when this body shall cease to be. And yet there is an entity of which there was never a time when it was not, for which there shall never be a time when it shall not be. This spirit you are; there was never a time when this spirit was not. Just think of yourself going on and on into infinity, that there shall never be a time when this spirit shall cease to be. It will go on into infinity. So, what is this misery and fear in you?

It is possible for a terminal patient, if he has even three months left ahead of him, depending upon who is guiding and how he is being guided, to reach a point where that time for him can be extremely useful, even a joyful experience, an experience of centeredness. Because, what else is death, but an experience of centeredness?

The mind is a field of energy. This energy field has a core, a center, from which it operates, from where it extends out into the senses, into the neuro-muscular system, sensory and motor organs, internal organs and memories and brain functions and all the rest. It permeates them. At the hour of death it withdraws and returns to the center. This centeredness is death. That center, that point, is the one that migrates, like a spark, jumping across the gaps of space and time to another space-time-causation coordinate which is named another body. We call that reincarnating, getting into body again.

Bless God for our death! We can experience meditation at least once a life! And we can get centered. If you would not center yourself happily throughout this life, then you've no alternative but be forced to be centered at least once. But if you do it happily throughout life, through meditation, then when the real time for a final centeredness comes, you are treading familiar territory; you are quite happy.

So if a doctor knows this person will live for three months or six months . . . you know, this person is now not going about his normal business in life. He is not a busy man. He has all the time in the world. In six months he can achieve miracles. Let him learn to die with dignity, with peace, with quiet, with centeredness. Teach him the art of meditation, and through that meditation he will find reduction in physical pain also. Even if he does not find reduction in physical pain, he will learn to accept it to a certain degree. So that at least we have alleviated a little of the mental suffering, self-pity and resignation attached to it. He has something to look forward to through that centeredness, the promise of a light, the fact that the longer you can use that part of the mind which is still alert, the closer you are going to be in touch with the light within, the Christ within, the thousand suns described in the Gita.

The terminal patient is in an ideal position to learn the art of relaxation, meditation, mental withdrawal. He cannot say, "Hey, you are teaching me to withdraw from life!" His withdrawal from life is a fact already accepted. Let him use that time.

But yet the artificial prolonging of the body which, for all practical purposes, is already gone—that makes no sense in this context. I would rather have someone make me sit up and let me take my deep final breaths and go. If I am really incapacitated in a hospital bed, I would, of course, be certain that I would not continue in this body, or that this body would not continue with me. I would like to be taken down from the bed and helped to sit on the floor with a meditation cushion, no matter what the amount of discomfort, to keep my spine straight and take my few breaths, irrespective of what medical effect it has on the body; I would like to die in the state of meditation.

Question: Some people are not in any position to make any decision!

Answer: Well, let us make our decisions now.

NOTES
CHAPTER 2

1.   To understand this seemingly odd expression please refer to the discussion of the yoga concept of time in chapter four.

Why Grieve over the Body?

The thoughts about preserving the body are not part of the yoga tradition. This transient entity which is composed of many elements must decompose. Seeing a death is to reach a state of *vairagya*, dispassion. Even if it is of the momentary "dispassion at the cremation ground," *(shmashaana-vairagya)*, of the kind experienced by Kabir's companions, it still leaves us with a reminder to search for the immortal spiritual Self. This is illustrated by the follow-Self conquers the three worlds. Let us go and receive this Progenitor, God the Father of the world, had two groups of children: the devas and the asuras, the good ones and the bad ones, the forces of goodness and the forces of evil, the gods and the demons. These two groups were fighting with each other for the conquest and mastery of the three worlds. Prajapati sent out an announcement to the three worlds:

> There is an entity called the self: this self is free of hunger, free of disease: this self is free of sorrow and

grief, it is immortal, it is all-knowing, never-born, never dying, it has no darkness and no ignorance. He who knows this self, conquers the three worlds.

Each of the two sides, the good ones and the bad ones, heard the announcement and asked among themselves, What is this secret weapon? He who knows this Self conquers the three worlds. Let us go and receive this knowledge from him and we will conquer the three worlds. Both sides thus held their separate conferences. The evil ones sent a representative named Virochana, which means "the glamorous one." The devas sent their king, Indra, which means "the masterful one." So the Masterful One and the Glamorous One both went out to study under Prajapati, God the Progenitor. When they went there, Prajapati, God the Progenitor, asked, "What do you want?"

"Well, we have heard this announcement from you and we have been sent here by our respective parties to come and learn from you about the Self."

Prajapati said, "All right, but I cannot teach it just like this. You have to live a life of *brahmacharya*, celibacy, walking in God, control and discipline, for thirty-six years here in my ashram and I will tell you about it."

So for thirty-six years their beards, nails and hair grew, and they hardly looked like the original glamorous kingly selves. They practiced all kinds of disciplines and celibacy. After thirty-six years of service to the guru they approached the guru and said, "Sir, it is thirty-six years now. Will you please teach us about the Self?"

He said, "Oh yes. First go and take a good bath. Pare your nails. Shave, have a good meal and a drink. Put on good clothes."

They did accordingly.

"All right," Prajapati then said, "go take a look at your face in a bowl of water. How is it? Is it handsome?" They said, "Yes."

"Are you hungry? Are you thirsty?"

"No."

"Do you have any sorrow, grief, trouble right now?"

"No, sir."

"You know the Self, now. Get out!"

So Indra and Virochana both went out from Prajapati's ashram very happily to report to the respective parties about this self. Virochana, the Glamorous One, who represented the demonic forces, went all the way back and told his party: "Oh, this was nothing. I don't know why Prajapati wasted my thirty-six years when it is here, the body, beautiful, handsome; keep it well fed, keep it well adorned. This is the Self, take care of it."

So the Upanishads, the texts from the 12th or 13th century B.C. go on to say that up to this day, the descendants of the demons still honor the corpse; they sprinkle it with perfumes and dress it bountifully, trying to preserve it, thinking that this way the Self is being saved.

Indra returned to Prajapati from halfway and after many years of further study and discipline, experienced the true Self. (Chandogya Upanishad 8. 7-15).

There are religions in which a great many rituals and ceremonies are performed for the dead. The Chinese, with the great Confucian tradition behind them of making yearly offerings to the spirits of the ancestors, have people going out to the graves and laying flowers. Also among the

Catholics, there is the All Souls Day. So also in India, on the thirteenth day, a ceremony called *shraddha* is performed in which food offerings are made. Also once a year for fifteen days the entire country celebrates a commemoration of this type.

In the Roman Catholic Church there is a Mass for the peace of the soul after death and sometimes people commemorate the anniversary with a similar celebration of the Mass.

There is always this controversy among the Catholics, the Chinese, the Indians or wherever there is this feeling to commemorate the dead, as to how much of this is really for our mental satisfaction and whether it is possible that these rituals and ceremonies really bring any kind of solace or peace or well being for the one who is already departed. Sometimes it is believed that whatever offerings are made at such occasions are converted into a spiritual essence that reaches the spirit. Whether that is so, we have no way of knowing. But what does matter is that some kind of a statement of the sublime must be made to the human psyche. It is a fact that death wipes out all debts—but only the ones between us and the departed. At the same time we need to let death be our reminder about the debts we have yet to pay, lest we die unhappy and carry a psychic burden along to the realms beyond.

When people have come back home from the cremation, they take a bath and wash off the feelings of sadness. In the bereaved home a ritual fire is burnt and a special fumigation ceremony is performed: the powder incense which is a mixture of perhaps a hundred herbs mixed with *ghee,* the clarified butter, is offered into the flames with recitation of highly uplifting mantras whose precise and sophisticated intonation alone charms the mind away from one's grief. The *samagri*, the powder mixture of incense herbs has been tested in scientific laboratories. It is germicidal and fungicidal and highly air-freshening without causing any ecological imbalance. The neighbors bring food for the bereaved home, and make certain that the family members eat.

On the second day after the cremation, the relatives go to the cremation ground and gather the charred remains from the wood ashes. The bones are bleached white by the fire, light like flowers, none larger than petals. The ceremony is called "gathering flowers." All these flowers fit into a bag the size of a pillow case. These are the true ashes of the body. There are no ashes in a burial; one wonders where the thought of "ashes to ashes" originated. These ashes, the flowers, are taken to a river, and are surrendered to the flowing waters with a few prayer offerings, together with some garden flowers. All the personal belongings, such as the horoscope, eyeglasses and clothing are all surrendered to the waters. That evening—or if the river is a distant journey, then upon the party's return—there is a quiet gathering of friends in the home. This is the last time that grief is a public sharing. Thereafter one continues with the normal duties of life. In many cultures throughout the world there is a feast in the memory and honor of the dead, after a certain number of days or even a whole year. In some cultures the dead bodies are not put away out of the city. You go down to places like Samoa or South America for example, where the graves are right in the families' courtyard and they are beautifully adorned and better painted than the houses. As it were, the spirit remains part of the family. This has a desirable effect on the family, community and the society in several ways. One, the people are in this way trained to an emotion of modesty and humility because they practice reverence toward the elders. Two, they recognize the karmic debts owed toward their predecessors and pay these debts to the succeeding generations. Three, they are constantly reminded that death is not far away and that the boundary lines between this world and the next are imaginary and artificial.

However, we repeat that the thoughts about preserving the body are not part of the yoga tradition. Here, let me explain further the yoga view of body, and some contemplations regarding the body.

> some flesh to eat,
> a beautiful woman,
> and a corpse—
> so the same body is seen three ways,
> by a wolf,
> a passionate youth,
> and a yogi.
> —a Sanskrit verse

According to our *samskaras* and consequent attitudes, we see the same object or entity in many different ways. What may be some flesh to devour in the eye of a hungry wolf is a sex object to another kind of "wolf." The yogi is a master of the corpse posture and recognizes his own body to be but a corpse that has been made alive through the presence of a spiritual force. To such a yogi the same attractive female is similarly a corpse. To a yogini, a handsome male is a corpse. The yogi immediately wants to go to the source of that beauty which is reflecting in the cheeks and the eyes. He wishes to touch the eternal beauty of the soul, and sees the body merely as a shroud that is torn easily. He pays much attention to this body to keep it fit. Through rigorous practice of hatha yoga and internal cleansing, he makes the body function as perfectly as possible. He continuously revitalizes it with *prana*; establishes full control over it so that it may be a fit instrument for sitting in *samadhi*, for the service of others, and for the mission of teaching the world. For the body itself, he has no great attraction or attachment. He does not associate it with his "I."

It is not that I have a soul. Rather, I am a soul; I have a body. The Sanskrit word for body, *deha*, is derived from the verb *dih*, "to smear, to anoint." When we are mentally attached to the body and consider it to be our ego, our personality, it becomes nothing but a smear, a stain. This very body when properly understood also anoints the soul. It is the chrism. How unfortunate that we remember only the chrism but have forgotten the Christ within.

This body is a composition of five elements: earth, water, fire, air, space. What is composed, must decompose. One of the Sanskrit words for creation is *panchi-karana*, bringing the five together; and a word for death is *panchatva*, returning the five to their origins. The soul neither goes nor comes. People often ask: Where does the soul go after death? Coming and going can be attributed to material objects in space. The spirit does not dwell in a spacial or temporal dimension. The question is irrelevant. The soul is not composed of many; only the body is. Looking at this unreliable body whose very continuity is doubtful the very next moment, the yogi finds no reason for pride in the fleeting youth. He despairs of ever making this heap of chemicals completely clean. When one looks at the body alone, without the spirit, without life—what remains but foulness? One comes face to face with death. Reader, if you have not the courage to look at the body as it will be three days or three months after death, do not read the rest of this chapter.

The yogis of all orders, at one time or another, undergo special training regarding a discipline to overcome attachment of the body. A disciple may be advised to sit in a cemetery, on a grave, even right on a corpse, all night, for many nights, and practice his prayers and meditations. As we shall see in the laya yoga contemplations, he learns to dissolve his body-ego.

Here I would like to refer to the most important Buddhist meditation manual of the Southern School, known as Theravada, the Path of the Elders. This manual entitled *Visuddhimagga*, the Path of Purification, was written by the great venerable monk, Buddhaghosa, in the fifth century, A.D. It is remarkable for its detail and the passages quoted here may seem somewhat extreme to the uninitiated but sooner or later those initiated into spiritual life arrive at these very contemplations.[1]

> As the Elder, Vangias, was wandering for alms, it seems soon after going forth, lust arose in him on seeing a woman. Thereupon he said to the venerable Ananda:
> "I am afire with sensual lust
> And burning flames consume my mind;
> In pity tell me, Gotama,
> How to extinguish it for good."
> The Elder said,

"You do perceive mistakenly,
That burning flames consume your mind.
Look for no sign of beauty there,
For that it is which leads to lust.
See foulness there and keep your mind
Harmoniously concentrated;
Formations see as alien,
As ill, not self, so this great lust
May be extinguished, and no more
Take fire thus ever and again."
The Elder expelled his lust and then went on with his
alms round.   —I. 103

Meditation subjects are of two kinds, that is, generally useful meditation subjects and special meditation
subjects.
Herein, loving kindness towards the Community of
Bhikkus etc., and also mindfulness of death are what
are called generally useful meditation subjects. Some
say perception of foulness, too.   —III.57

The ten kinds of foulness (of the body) are these:
the bloated, the livid, the festering, the cut-up,
the gnawed, the scattered, the hacked and scattered, the bleeding, the worm-infested, and a skeleton.
                                                  —III. 105

The sixth chapter of the text goes into detail of the
methods for such contemplation. The yogi finds the corpse
in such states and sits or stands, watching intently; he
visualizes his own body in such states. He is, however,
warned to undertake such practices only under strict
control of the teacher. Details are provided as which of the
ten foulness contemplations are suitable for whom:

And individually the bloated suits one who is greedy
about shape since it makes evident the disfigurement
of the body's shape. The livid suits one who is greedy
about the body's color since it makes evident the
disfigurement of the skin's color. The festering (194)
suits one who is greedy about the smell of the body

aroused by scents, perfumes, etc., since it makes
evident the evil smells connected with this sore,
the body. The cut up suits one who is greedy about
compactness in the body since it makes
evident the hollowness inside it.   —VI. 85

And repulsive as this object is, still it arouses joy and
happiness in him by his seeing its advantages, thus
"Surely in this way I shall be liberated from aging
and death," and by his abandoning the hindrances'
oppression; just as a garbage heap does in a flower-
scavenger by his seeing the advantages, thus, "Now
I shall get a high wage," and as the workings of
purges and emetics do in a man suffering the pains
of sickness.   —VI. 87

Among the thirty-eight objects of concentration
and contemplation, including the ten foulness contemplations, there are four practices of mindfulness:
Recollection (or mindfulness) of death, mindfulness
occupied with the body, mindfulness of breathing
and recollection of peace.   —III. 105

The mindfulness of death and of being occupied
with the body is a prerequisite for total mastery of
the mindfulness of breathing. Here is a simile. Sup-
pose a hunter wanted to catch a monkey that lived
in a grove of thirty-two palms, and he shot an arrow
through a leaf of the palm that stood at the beginning and gave a shout; then the monkey went
leaping successively from palm to palm till it reached
the last palm; and when the hunter went there too
and did as before, it came back in like manner to
the first palm; and being followed thus again and
again, after leaping from each place where a shout
was given, it eventually jumped on to one palm
and firmly seizing the palm shoot's leaf spike in the
middle, would not leap any more even when shot—
so it is with this.   —VIII. 68

The application of the simile is this. The thirty-two
parts of the body are like the thirty-two palms in
the grove. The monkey is like the mind. The meditator

is like the hunter. The range of the meditator's mind in the body with its thirty-two parts as object is like the monkey's inhabiting the palm grove of thirty-two palms. The settling down of the meditator's mind in the last part after going successively (from part to part) when he began by giving his attention to head hairs is like the monkey's leaping from palm to palm and going to the last palm, (246) when the hunter shot an arrow through the leaf of the palm where it was and gave a shout. Likewise in the return to the beginning. His doing the preliminary work on those parts that have appeared, leaving behind those that did not appear while, as he gave his attention to them again and again, some appeared to him and some did not, is like the monkey's being followed and leaping up from each place where a shout is given. The meditator's repeated attention given to the part that in the end appears the more clearly of any two that have appeared to him and his finally reaching absorption, is like the monkey's eventually stopping in one palm, firmly seizing the palm shoot's leaf spike in the middle and not leaping up even when shot. —VIII. 69

What is intended here as Mindfulness Occupied with the Body is the thirty-two aspects. This meditation subject is taught as the direction of attention to repulsiveness thus:

Again, bhikkhus, a bhikkhu reviews this body, up from the soles of the feet and down from the top of the hair and contained in the skin as full of many kinds of filth thus: In this body there are head hairs, body hairs, nails, teeth, skin, flesh sinews, bones, bone-marrow, kidney, heart, liver, midriff, spleen, lights, bowels, entrails, gorge, dung, bile, phlegm, pus, blood, sweat, fat, tears, grease, spittle, snot, oil of the joints, and urine (M iii, 90), the brain being included in the bone marrow in this version (with a total of only thirty-one aspects). —VIII. 44

These contemplations are, as we have said earlier,

common to all meditative traditions. A disciple is often ordered to spend some nights meditating in a cemetery or a cremation ground. This is also a prerequisite for the vows of Swamihood. Some Tantric trainees may be required to sit on a corpse for many nights of mantram practice. Ashes from the cremation pyre are applied to the body so that one is reminded that this living body, too, with all its temptations, distractions and pride, is virtually no more than ashes.

Death is as near to him as drying up is to rivulets in the summer heat, as falling is to the fruits of trees when the sap reaches their attachments in the morning, as breaking is to clay pots tapped by a mallet, as vanishing is to dew drops touched by the sun's rays. Hence it is said:

> The nights and days go slipping by
> As life keeps dwindling steadily
> Till mortals' span, like water pools
> In failing rills, is all used up
> As there is fear, when fruits are ripe,
> That in the morning they will fall,
> So mortals are in constant fear,
> When they are born, that they will die.
> And as the fate of pots of clay
> Once fashioned by the potter's hand,
> Or small or big or baked or raw,
> Condemns them to be broken up,
> So mortals' life leads but to death
> The dew drop on the blade of grass
> Vanishes when the sun comes up;
> Such is a human span of life;
> So, mother, do not hinder me.
>   —VII. 12

A bhakkhu develops mindfulness of death thus, "Oh, let me live as long as it takes to breathe in and breathe out, or as long as it takes to breathe out and breathe in that I may attend to the Blessed One's teaching, surely much could be done by me." These are called bhikkhus who dwell in diligence and keenly develop mindfulness of death for the destruction of cankers.   —VIII. 37

The body reflects the universe on a reduced scale.

yad brahmande tat pinde,
yat pinde tad brahmande.
Whatever is in the universe is in the body;
Whatever is in the body is in the universe.

We read in the Puranas that each entity of the universal reality can be found in the body and personality. The seven lower worlds starting from the feet upwards, seven upper worlds starting from the navel upwards.

In the sound chakra (nada chakra) dwells the sun
In the point chakra (bindu) dwells the moon
In the eyes dwells Mars; in the heart Mercury,
In the forehead dwells Jupiter; in sexual hormones
   Venus
In the navel Saturn, in the mouth Rahu, in the feet
   Ketu
And thus all the planets are in this very body,
divided in proportion from soles of the feet to the
head; and those who are born in this world must
eventually die, there is no doubt about it.
               —Garuda-Purana, Part 2, Ch. 22, v. 63-66

All the cycles of the universe are revolving in the body as we shall see again in our study of the signs of impending death and in the beginning steps of the laya yoga method. Beyond such cycles is the spiritual realm of the Conscious Self that declares:

I am not the body nor the body is mine.
                    —Ashtavakra-Gita, Ch. 2, v. 22

The separation of the two principles—the Conscious Self and the corpse-like body that borrows life from Self— is inevitable. The yogis sing:

My friendly bird, a flying one!

Who can trust you?
There are nine windows in this cage
and all the doors are open.
Your coming is improbable; flying away very easy.
For your sake the palaces have been built;
sons, wealth and wife—all of these
you leave, you loveless one, and you flee.
I may build a castle;
I may build a citadel;
I may erect a thousand dams, says Brahmananda,
You are so crafty you will still find your way out.
                              —Songs of Brahmananda

Often we come face to face with the fact of body's
impermanence. Said Milton:

How soon hath the subtle thief of youth
Stolen on his wings my three and twentieth year!

So we hear an anonymous Sanskrit poet say:

Earth is burned to cinders, the Mount Meru
    scatters to the winds.
Even the ocean dries up, such is this world.
Do you expect permanence to your body?

We are reminded in the Garuda-Purana:

Impermanent, unsteady, with no base,
made up simply of juices in this body.
In this body made of lumps of food,
what good qualities can there be?

The food cooked in the morning vanishes by
    the evening.
What is permanent in such a body made of
    juices that spoil so easily?
                              Part 2, Ch. 13, v. 14, 15

But to the last minute our expectations and consequent
frustrations remain with us:

The face has all wrinkled, the hair has turned grey;
the limbs are worn and weak, craving alone is yet
    youthful.
                    —Shrngara-shataka of Bhartrhari, 14

This craving will continue to drop us down when the spirit is ready to go aloft. So we are reminded by the yogis constantly to recognize and remember the impermanence of this body. Like *moha-mudgara*, the mace to beat the delusion with—a song sung to great Shankara—we hear even the yogis of today sing:

> Awake traveler and watch;
> The trumpet of departure is now blowing
> All night has been spent sleeping
> and now it is dawn.
> All your companions have already gone.
> Why sleep in your eyes?
> —Songs of Brahmananda

Be mindful of the impermanence of this body and meditation will come easily to you. But more of this under laya yoga.

Every pious householder on the yoga path daily applies a pinch of ashes on his forehead and on other parts of his body. These ashes are specially prepared by burning an appropriate mixture of herbs in sacred fires and also have therapeutic value for the skin. The formula is recited:

> The fire—it is ashes.
> The air—it is ashes.
> The waters—it is ashes.
> The ground—it is ashes.
> The space—it is ashes.
> All this (phenomenal world) is ashes.
> The mind and these eyes (i.e., cognitive senses)
> are ashes.

What many yogis do daily, the Catholics also do once a year on Ash Wednesday.

At one time while living in England this author asked a friend visiting India to bring him some ashes from a cremation ground. When these ashes were borne on the body, for weeks all physical passions subsided and a sense of spiritual ecstasy reigned. We have seen philosophers like Plato, Nietzche, Heidegger and Sartre agree with the Puranas which say:

> What you will do at the hour of death,
> do that very act daily.[2]

The application of ashes is one such daily reminder of death, a great emancipation from bodily preoccupations, a symbol recognizing that training for death has already begun. The first step in this training is to modify our attitudes toward the body.

Here a word of warning. There are many people who have the hobby of collecting mantras and teaching from books and heresay, because collecting stamps, antiques and coins is somewhat more expensive! Please do not rush into these practices from the book. Buddhagosa warns:

> . . . when a meditator wants to develop the ghana . . .
> he should in the way already described approach a
> teacher of the kind mentioned . . . and learn the
> meditation subject from him . . .
> . . . he should not go there at once, like one who
> plunges into a river where there is no ford.
> —The Path of Purification, Vol. 1, VI.6. p. 186

What we are writing here is a description of what is taught by a Master, and not the prescription for one who has not yet surrendered his ego to a qualified guru. Or else, he will subject himself to many disorders of the mind. An average householder practices only the milder forms of these contemplations. Through the practice of these, by adopting them in our attitudes, (1) we slowly prepare ourselves for the initiatory death with which true conquest over death begins, and meanwhile, (2) we learn not to be overcome by grief.

Of grief, a few words need to be said. One need not conform to the conventions of a civilization and merely wipe corners of the eyes. Open crying is a great relief. Throughout the Old Testament we read of wailing and much rending of clothes at the hour of grief. Even today, from Greece to India, as soon as people come within earshot of the bereaved home, they begin a wailing song, much as they sing joyfully as they approach a house when someone is born. Professional mourners are employed so that those who might otherwise choke back their tears and suffer a silent shock would in this way find a release. So far as such emotions are concerned it is better not to repress them. Today our civilization is passing through a process in which no naturalness is encouraged. The funeral homes are made to look like palaces and certain formalities must be followed even to express grief! The end result is permanent psychological damage. Grief of all kinds turns into suppressed rage and then into a mute depression. The poor victims of such civilizing process then must visit a psychologist who will teach for fifty dollars an hour how to beat a pillow to relieve one's hidden tensions! In the more traditional cultures a spontaneous expression flows naturally.

An emotion cannot be suppressed successfully, its poison eats one's very innards and leads to all manner of mental and physical illness. However, as Gurudev H. H. Swami Rama says: an emotion can be replaced with a positive thought and the discriminative wisdom enlightens the burdened mind.

When the human in us weeps, the wise elders, swamis, spiritual teachers all urge us to curb our feelings.

So long as the feelings are present we will continue to pour them out but we need to replace the feelings with genuine wisdom. Once you have expressed that grief, do not carry on with it. Now turn your back to it and break the straw.

In India there is a tradition: They say, do not grab on to the soul who no longer belongs to your time zone. Do not try to hook it and pull it down. For example: no one ever goes out shopping for the child until after it is born. Nothing ever is prepared for the child, not even any clothing. A piece of the mother's sari is torn to wrap around the baby. The naming is done eleven days after. The baby is not yours yet. His consciousness is still way back where he has come from. This is life after death. A part of his being is still way back beyond his past death. Why would you be in such a hurry to pull his consciousness down here with your thoughts of this time zone. Let him be. Let him gradually wean himself from the awareness of all kinds of traumas that remains hidden at the unconscious level. God knows where he is coming from and you are in such a rush to bring him to your time zone and make him your possession! For the first few days the child should remain absolutely possessionless. For eleven days the child does not even need a name in this time zone.

Similarly at death we are advised to let go, not to let our grief create tormenting ropes to tie down the psychic energies of the departed. Let him be free. With this in view, we are told:

> One should rather sprinkle milk at the spot of death
> (or on the cremation ground)
> and sprinkle water in the memory of the departed
> one but not shed tears.
> The departed one is helpless and has to swallow

the phlegm and tears poured by the grieving
relatives; therefore do not cry at his death.
Simply perform the rites
according to one's strength and means.
                    —Garuda Purana, Part II. Ch. 5, v. 56, 57

A reading of the second chapter of the Bhagavad-
Gita alleviates much burden of grief. Understand the
immortality of the self and consider the body a garment
to be cast off:

As one removes old garments and puts on new ones,
so does the master of the body take off the worn
flesh to wear the new one.   —II. 22

We hear the same thought echoing from Kahlil Gibran:

For what is it to die but to stand naked in the wind
and to melt into the sun?
And what is it to cease breathing but to free the
breath from its restless tides, that it may rise and
expand and seek God unencumbered?
. . . A little while, a moment of rest upon the wind,
and another woman shall bear me.
                    —The Prophet

Lord Krishna of the Bhagavad-Gita impresses on
Arjuna the infinite existence of the Spiritual Being that we
are:

(because) What is not, shall never be
What is, shall never cease to be . . .
                                —II. 16

The wise ones grieve neither for the living nor for
the dead.   —II.11

Contradictory statements above! Do not withhold
your wail and a cry. Yet, the wise do not grieve! Which
advice are we supposed to take to heart? Simply the advice
to be natural—and yet developing wisdom enough that a
certain dispassion develops, a certain faith arises in the
mind.

Where there is no one to comfort you, the Infinite within is our Guide and solace. We do not ever ask for such solace, for, Kabir says:

> The savour of wandering in the ocean of deathless life has rid me of all my asking:
> As the tree is in the seed, so all diseases are in this asking.
> —Songs of Kabir, tr. Rabindranath Tagore

The true solace comes without any asking; only through a quiet surrender. This was once confirmed in my own life.

I used to live in a country called Guyana where I had an ashram. It was about 40 miles from the city, Georgetown, the capital. Half of the year there was no road. We used to get to the ashram rowing a boat. I had a post box in the city. I had left India in 1952, traveled around many countries and there I was in Guyana in 1958. I had not seen my father for a long time. One day I came to the city to collect my mail, opened the post box, and there was a cablegram which had been lying there for ten days, that my father had died. As a priest in the Hindu community, one of my traditional tasks is to go to people's homes when invited and conduct scripture readings. It is customary in Indian villages that on occasions such as births, marriages, religious initiations, (which are similar to baptisms and bar mitzvahs here) deaths, or just whenever a person or family so desires to do these special readings, it is done. Everybody from the community comes. Sometimes one thousand people are fed three times a day before the morning, afternoon and evening sessions! The readings sometimes go on for a day, three days, seven days. People are immersed in that kind of thought; feeding others, giving, sharing, listening and absorbing what they can. Children run around, all through the crowd; they are not separated from the adults. They always share the life with the elders. You listen to what you want to listen to. Let children be there. They are part of the world. The more you separate them from your life, the more you separate the old from your life. The more you separate the newborn, the more you separate the dying. It is the same process; you don't want to look into your past as children so you don't want to look back to your future as old men. You don't want the company of the children so you don't want the company of the old. Lock them all away! Bring them home from the hospital when they are born, put them in a separate room. So when you are old, they pick you up and put you in a separate senior citizens home. It is just the perfect law of karma; you die alone as your children slept alone when they were babies.

The roads were not well paved, and I was supposed to drive from Georgetown to a village about 110 miles, at a speed of 20 miles per hour, to do a reading of the Ramayana, which is the most popular scripture, the story of God's incarnation as Rama, the Ideal Man.

No one knew that I had received the cablegram of my father's death. I drove the 110 miles, arrived and prepared myself. The family had prepared a beautiful seat for me to teach from. I sat down and picked up the book to read. It is my habit; whenever I am to read from the Sanskrit scriptures I say a silent prayer, take the book in my hands and open it with my eyes closed. Wherever it opens, I read from there. So I sat, closed my eyes and opened the book.

The Prince, Rama, had been sent into exile because his stepmother wanted her own son to be crowned King. Her son, Bharata, heard that in order for him to be crowned, his older brother, who was the rightful heir to the throne, had to be exiled with his wife. And in that grief, their father had died. Bharata vowed not to sit on that throne but rather go in search of his elder brother. Into the forests he went.

The passage that opened in front of me started thus:

All savings end in spending,
All risings end in falling;
All unions end in separation,
All living ends in dying.
As a fruit ripens on the tree
has no other fear nor another
danger, but that of falling.

So, my brother Bharata, to a human being once born, there is no other fear, no other danger but that of death. All other fears and dangers are attendant upon that one. People greet each other at the turn of the season not realizing that season by season by season their own lifespans are now being curtailed. Every morning they see the sun rise and rejoice in its beauty; every evening they see the sun set and are happy sharing the view, not thinking that another day, yet another day has been reduced in the lifespan. But remember, oh Bharata, remember we are all going in the same direction.

As two pieces of wood floating in the river, touched by the action of waves and winds from two different places, float together for a little while, so, human beings, touched by the winds and waves of their own karma, action, come together for a while, float together and then go their own separate ways.

Oh Bharata, as a man walking on the pavement sees another going in a chariot pulled by fast steeds and the man on the pavement waves to the man in the chariot saying, "You go along, I too am coming on foot." So my brother, our father has gone on a chariot pulled by fast steeds, but we too are going the same way.

Where I had no one to share my grief, it was the invisible hand of Grace that opened the book for me so that as it were, I would hear Rama's words. Have faith, and surrender to Grace, the pall of grief will be uplifted.

When I read these passages to the people, no one could understand why I was so moved. But there was a spirit there that had opened the page to console me.

It is from such experiences that I say to the grief-stricken: let God console you.

Once the Buddha was preaching a sermon. An old widow came named Kisa Gotami. Her five year old child, her only link with her dead husband, died. Then someone told her, "Kisa, the Buddha is not far away. He can do something to relieve your grief or perhaps even bring the child to a new life."

So she went to the Buddha with the corpse in her arms, laid it down before him and said, "Lord, people tell me that you might revive the child or give me something so that I might not suffer such grief."

The Buddha replied, "I will indeed revive your child, Kisa, but first I need one small thing. Would you go and bring me some rice grains or mustard seed?"

She got up to go and bring some rice grains from her home. The Buddha, however, added, "There is one stipulation; you cannot bring it from your own home but from some other home where no one has died."

Kisa went to the neighbor and said, "Some rice

grains, please!"

"Why do you want them from me; why do you not take them from your own home?"

Kisa said, "The Buddha has stipulated that they come from a home where no one has died."

The lady said, "But we had a death here three years ago. And he died in such and such circumstances, and it was so painful, and we were so grieving."

Kisa listened to the story of grief and went to the next neighbor, and yet another neighbor throughout the whole village. She went from village to village with the resolve, "I must bring some rice grains from a home where no one has died." In the process she heard so many stories from so many grief-sticken families that she forgot her own grief. She returned to the Buddha empty-handed.

"Did you bring the rice grains?"

"No," she answered, "I could find no home where no one had died. But you have relieved my grief."

According to great Shankara, grief is the burning in the mind caused by frustration of many expectations. A wise man overcomes it right in this life. The sin is the differentiation between good and evil, and the knots of the cave are the knots of ignorance in the heart. When ignorance about our spiritual nature vanishes, we make our lives a preparation for death and the transcendent existence beyond. We may be attached to our possessions but we need to remind ourselves:

> Daily the living beings are seen carried way by death;
> yet others intend to stay here—there can be nothing
> more strange.   —Mahabharata

When an entire civilization is devoted to hiding the

fact of death, our fear of death and the grief at its presence is constantly strengthened. The yoga teaching reminds us that when we no longer try to keep death out of sight we learn to

> earn merit daily as though
> death holds one by the hair.
> —Manu

That's it.

The idea is that attitude building is important; not merely what you do at the hour of death but what you have been doing while you are alive. These stories give us a philosophy of life. Read them; hear them. They indicate what others have done. How they have been inspired.

It is now and not later that one should resolve to use this body to pursue liberation of the spirit. We read in the Puranas:

> While this body is yet free of disease and
> the old age is yet far away
> While the strength in the senses yet waxes and
> the lifespan is not in ebb,
> the wise man must right now undertake
> endeavors for spiritual uplifting
> for, what effort to dig a well
> when the house is already on fire.

Therefore we pray:

> May the royal swan of my mind, Lord,
> play at thy lotus feet now, today;
> When the pranas are departing
> and the throat is choked
> with phlegm, bile and wind—
> how will I ever call upon thee?

We see the same sentiment expressed in the Psalms of David (6):

> My soul, O save me, for thy goodness sake!
> For in death no remembrance of thee;
> Who in grave can celebrate thy praise?

Let the occasion of death be a reminder of God.

NOTES
CHAPTER 3

1.   The quotations are from the translation of Bhikkhu Nyanamoli, Shamb-
     hala, 1976.

2.   This is quoted so often in the oral tradition that the original source can
     no longer be traced.

Actions and Transitions

ACTIONS

One very important belief is common in the yoga tradition—that our last thought governs our next life. Whatever the last thoughts of a dying person, that is his next life. This is not so strange as we now know of the similarity of the birth and waking up, death and falling asleep. It comes from a tradition in which birth is not the composition nor death a termination because the whole universe is seen as a cycle, a world view which has nothing to do with a linear concept of time. One cycle is the life span of a Brahma, a world-soul, in terms of 36,000 cycles of creation and dissolutions of all the universes. When one's thinking about the time-spams is on that scale, the idea of becoming attached to sixty or seventy years is childish. There is nothing so important in a period of seventy years that one has to really grieve after it. Seventy years is really a speck of dust in the Universal Consciousness, in the Universal Person. The World Soul is said to live for 100 years, defined as 100 years of the Brahma, the World-Soul; and one cycle of the creation and dissolution of the whole universe is a single day. So, one lunar month is one day and a night for a resident of the moon. A solar year is a day and a night in terms of the northern and southern equinox. Thus, again, one whole cycle of creation and dissolution of the entire universe, billions upon billions of light years, that entire period is a single day and night in the light of Brahma, the World-Soul, and that Brahma lives for a hundred years, that is, 36,000 cycles of creation and dissolution. So it is with the time scale of an ant or a bug as compared to my time scale; my time scale as compared to that of a *deva,* a shining one. When the universe is dissolved the World-Soul loses its body. How much it has to lose, billions and billions of planets, but, it has no more to lose than I! It depends entirely how you view the world, what you see, what ratio you are thinking of, what relationships you have. It is in terms of a cell in the human body as compared to a planet in the body of the World-Soul. Even at that scale the death is nothing. It is simply a dissolution of the organism, not a dissolution of the spirit. Even a day of Brahma consisting of 36,000 cycles of creation and dissolution is insufficient to satisfy a human's desire for a long lifespan. Brahma dies in a day of Vishnu, Vishnu in a day of Shiva, and even Shiva vanishes after a million cycles of creations and dissolutions.

In this chain of cycles there is an ancient Indian symbol of an insect caught in a frog's mouth, the frog in a snake's fangs, the snake gathered by a pouncing eagle. Only he who has terminated his attachment to time and, consequently, to space and causation becomes immortal. So when you view the universe in terms of these cycles, then you see that Einstein's theory of curved spaces comes true because those outer spaces are curved around the gravity pole. If the spaces are curved then the time too is curved, and somewhere along the line, the entire time must curve back around itself. If spaces are curved around the bodies that exert gravity pull, and here we think of the curving of the universal space, then we cannot escape that physics even touches the mystery of time and some day the physicists will confirm what some suspect: that time curves back upon itself and that everything is therefore a cycle. An end is the renovation, a new beginning. What is true of the whole cycle of the World-Soul, so also it is true of the cycles around the individual soul, as well as the cycles within cycles within cycles: the cycles of day and night, the cycles of sleep and wakefulness, the cycles of rising of the sun in the right nostril and the rising of the moon in the left nostril. That being the case, if we understand the difference between wakefulness and sleeping to a greater degree we can understand the difference between death and rebirth. Also for this reason night was regarded as the goddess of death in some ancient mythologies.

Now if you have learned the habit of watching your thoughts, watch your last thought at the moment of falling asleep; if you can somehow remember this last thought that trails off as you fall asleep you will find that it is where your first thought begins the next morning. Whatever type of mood you go to sleep in that is the first mood you start the day with. There is absolutely no doubt about it. There is no break in human thought from the moment when the mother and the father thoughts united and created, procreated, a fresh, new germinal thought in the tiny body that is then attached to the mother's womb. From that moment to the last thought of a human being at the hour of death there is no break whatsoever. It is one long single unbroken sentence. The longest sentence that can ever be written is this life-long one that we all are in the process of writing. There has never been any break, never even a "period" to break that thought. It ends only when the brain ceases to function. Even then there is doubt as to whether it ceases or still continues. So in order to have a good day tomorrow, have a good night tonight. In order to have a beautiful thought the whole day tomorrow, have a beautiful last thought tonight.

In order to have a beautiful last thought tonight have a beautiful thought the whole day today. Because the last thought of tonight is the gathered force, the sum total of all the thoughts of today. And all the thoughts of today are the continuation of the momentum you gave them first thing this morning which, again, was a continuation of where you left off last night which is again a vehicle of the potency of all the thoughts of yesterday. In this sentence there may be commas but hardly ever any semicolons. There are phrases and clauses within the sentence but there are no periods, no full stops. One thought leads into another thought very, very gently. There is a curving but hardly ever a sudden shift, hardly ever any right angles. If that is true, if our thoughts continue from day to day, from sleep to next wakefulness to the next sleep, then it is also true that death is not anything abrupt, is not even a break. The forces have been gathered over a long period of time.

Even our diseases we select twenty years before we get sick. A person of age twenty-five has already selected the disease he will have at the age of forty-five; he has already started the emotional momentum that will create the warp in his prana, that will in turn produce a warp in the cellular energy field. It takes time. It is a build-up and we wake up some morning, suddenly ill. Not really so suddenly. The dying person needs to know where he is. It is a continuation.

Question: Is the state of no-thought in meditation a comma?

Answer: For most people, there is no such thing as the state of no-thought in meditation. You see, you go into meditation also very gently, and you always carry one single thought that you concentrate on. Meditation has been described by Gurudev Swami Rama as one continuous thought. You maintain that thought which leads to a period of silence; yes, I would say that would be like a semicolon. A rest. But then when you come out of meditation again, like a large majority of people, you pick up where you had left off. The mood about it is now different because of the intervening meditation. The interpretation has changed. You may have sat down to meditate after a quarrel with your wife. The thought of your wife continues for a while during meditation and there are ups and downs in meditation. Then you go into the thought that has been assigned to you, be it breath, a word, a mantra. So you come to silence and restfulness. When you return from the deeper levels of the mind to the shallows, you pick up the thought of your wife but now you have brought in some peacefulness from the depths and then when you are thinking of the wife you are thinking of some of the fond things that you enjoyed before and you come down out of the meditation and are more inclined to give her a smile. It is like traveling, coming to a body of water, taking a dip, coming out on the other side and continuing on the path. Now I have said that that is so in the case of the majority but there is a minority of great masters who know how to suspend the entire activity of the conscious and the subconsicous mind. They are able to go into voluntary death symptoms.

Just as the last thought of the hour of sleep is the accumulation of all the thoughts that we have had during the day, and the mood we have carried, and then as we lie down and begin to go into introspection or a reverie before falling asleep, all of the day's events quickly pass before our eyes. At the hour of death also there follows this reverie. All the events of life are flashing past us and the last thought is not an independent thought.

There was an article many years ago in *Esquire* magazine, a very ignorant article by someone who wrote about a group of ladies talking and saying that:

> a person's last thought governs the kind of species in which he will reincarnate. So it appears that if, at the last hour of death a person were thinking of his cat, he should be born a cat!

That is certainly not the intent of the yoga tradition. We do not talk of particular thoughts but of the force of the sum total of karma, the sum total of the mental action of our whole lifetime. This sum total remains inside us, in the subtle body. Sometimes in the state of deep relaxation in the corpse posture, one is able to touch the fringes of the subtle body. In the storehouse of karma, all of this that we have done with our thoughts, words and actions is stored and its momentum is what carries us through.

If we have led a fairly undisciplined life then death is beyond our control. If we have not controlled the body, its urges, our food, sleep, sex, thoughts and fantasies of the body during our whole life, then we cannot control the functions of the body at the hour of death. If we have been creatures of momentary pleasure without the thought of the long term good, if there has been no discipline, the god of death comes licking his whiskers and says, here I am! But if there is even one single central thought in our life, we can stand and argue with death face to face. It does not matter what that central thought is, but there should be something positive. Not my success, not my pleasure, not my house, but something in which others are involved besides myself. Death is an otherness, because, you see, first you are one thing and then you are something else. Whatever you have clung to has to be wrenched away and whatever you have not clung to will not be wrenched away. Those who cling to themselves have to be wrenched away from themselves and that wrenching is terrible. May I narrate here a story from Mahabharata, the Sanskrit epic:

Savitri was a princess and Satyavan was an ashram boy and it was predicted that after one year of their marriage he would die. The mother and father were unwilling to marry their daughter to Satyavan, but Savitri had so much faith in herself, in her love, that she said: "I have chosen to marry him and that is it."

One day, exactly one year after the marriage, while gathering kindling for the evening ceremonial fire and other domestic use, Satyavan, the husband, complained of a headache. He lay down under a tree with his head in her lap. She sat there and kept the vigil. She saw the god of death approaching, which in Indian mythology is shown as riding a black buffalo, the dark beast of delusion. Here comes the god of death with a hook and a snare to catch the soul of Satyavan and to carry him away. He took Satyavan's soul and began to walk away. But Savitri would not go and leave him. She walked behind him. The god of death said to her:

"Well, I cannot take you. It is not your time yet. I did not come for you. You have to live the rest of your usual lifespan."

She replied, "A woman goes wherever her beloved husband goes. I married knowing that you would be coming one year later, knowing that I would argue with you and I will retrieve Satyavan's life back."

Death replies, "You loving woman, go on back. Nobody alive ever comes this far with me. This is not the way of the mortals who are still on earth."

She says, "No, but I have to come along."

They go on up to the sky and all the realms, and she keeps arguing. She is determined not to return without her husband.

Death says, "Well, you are making me break my own laws. Your will is very strong."

She says, "My love is very strong."

So he finally says, "All right, I cannot break my laws. Just ask for anything you want and I'll grant it to you, but just go back!"

She says, "What I want is a happy life with many children from my husband."

He has to keep his promise and in his way Savitri was able to defeat the god of death. Here is a married woman of whom the god of death was afraid. In the same way he was scared of Nachiketas, the great celibate. So you do not have to become a great monk to conquer death. There is the story of the conquest of death by a celibate who was initiated into the yoga meditative tradition. He lies at the gates of death for three days and three nights, and finally extracts all the knowledge of the art of life that he can from the mouth of death. Death tries to get out of it by offering him all kinds of favors. In the other story, it is an ordinary woman who goes after death and defeats him and brings her husband back alive. Then her husband wakes up from the sleep in his wife's lap and says,

"Honey, I had a dream. There was this terrible being riding a black buffalo who sent out a snare and hooked my soul and you walked behind us. You were arguing with him and brought me back here, and now I am awake."

So, if there is a single unselfishly central idea in your life, it will defeat the fear of death.[1]

There is the story of a martyr named Banda Bairagi in the history of India who was a great yogi but who joined the forces of those fighting against the tyrannical rulers of the time. He was captured with seven hundred of his followers and the rulers told him to convert, to change over to their religion. But he refused. So they cut off the heads of one hundred of his followers and put them on spikes, and affixed them around him with him in the center. They said, "Look, this is what has been done today and this is what we will do little by little to all of your followers."

In seven days all seven hundred of his followers were dead, their heads stuck on the spikes, and he was made to stand in the center. He was told, "Your turn is next."

Next day he was stripped bare and hot iron tongs were applied to pull off his flesh. He sat there with his eyes closed with a smile on his lips, without screaming, without showing any sign of pain and died.

There should be one thing that is central, that is unselfish, that is not for yourself, and if you have not maintained one such thought in your life then at least when you are sick, let something be done.

Those responsible should teach the sick to do some *japam*, some repetition, prayer, rosary, that they can occupy themselves with twenty-four hours, irrespective of the religion they belong to. We read in the scriptures:

> On whatever path people walk they come unto Me.
> Whatever form of Mine they worship
> Towards that very form I strengthen their faith
> And through that faith they come to Me.
> —Bhagavad Gita 4. 11; 7. 21

At the hour of death the Hindu sees the vision of Krishna or Vishnu or Shiva. The Muslims see Islamic symbols. The Greeks in the fourth century B.C. would see Zeus and other Greek gods. So did the ancient Egyptians see the Egyptian gods. The Christians see Virgin Mary, the saints or Christ. The Jews hear the Lord as they are supposed to. That is because God is not somewhere up in heaven. God is in our minds. She or He incarnates, taking from our minds the material for an incarnation. This is what the *Tibetan Book of the Dead* says: that whatever level of existence you are at, in that form you will see God or your Buddha. Very sick people sometimes see their dead ancestors coming and conversing with them.

So, whatever is the central faith of your being, let that faith become your vehicle and let it become alive. Let the last three months of a terminal patient be spent with a rosary. It does not matter whether it is a Muslim, a Hindu or a Christian rosary. Teach them to master the art of respiration, to exhale the prayer and inhale the prayer, and you will be surprised what happens to a terminal patient. Three months spent meditating, twelve hours a day—if you can help a person do that, the results will be absolutely amazing. So these mental preparations, if we have not undertaken them in life, they become extremely important before death.

As the hour of death approaches one begins to develop a child-like purity and innocence. A part of the mind again begins to believe. It begins to see what we saw as children. If some of the cobwebs can be removed, the inspired words can be spoken, the dying persons will really believe because they are now at the threshold. Nobody wants to think of the possibility of becoming absolutely *nihil*. No dying person is going to accept: I am going to be absolutely extinct; I shall completely cease to be. That is why we stress the importance of the second chapter of the Bhagavad-Gita that says:

That which exists shall never cease to be.

That which was not shall never come into being
From non-existence nothing comes. There is always pre-existence. There is always continuity of existence. The person who is dying is peeping through the window and is seeing the future and before he takes to sleep he wants to be prepared for it and he will listen. Do not clutter his mind with all kinds of worldly affairs at this time.

When one has led a life with certain basic disciplines, whatever those disciplines might be—a life of unselfishness, a life in which one has fulfilled one's karma, in which one has received and given unselfish love, a life that has not been built around contracts of one kind or another that are entered into at convenience and are broken licentiously, when in life there have been permanent relationships, when in life there have been unselfish commitments: where one has dared to commit himself to people and principles over long periods of time, then the person has learned to gather the potency of the thought force. Even if he has not reached total liberation he will be still better off at the hour of death than someone who has not lived such a life. Those who have not lived such a life, their death is absolutely involuntary. Their time has come and the body is deteriorating; their thoughts are still way back into the past, six years ago, seven years ago; vengefulness, sorrow, grief, self-pity permeates, makes them cry; their body completely unable to stand on its own. This is un-controlled, involuntary death. At the hour of death they have no direction.

But even though you have not been a great master yogi and cannot avert the force of karma or the hour of death, but you have led a pure life you can at that time take a certain control over the death process. You can sit up and give direction to your thoughts. You can die with the name of God on your mental lips. Take, for example, someone like Gandhi. If someone came and shot me, what would be my last cry? Amidst a crowd of thousands of people the assassin came tearing through the crowd with his hands joined in salute but with a pistol hidden in his palms. He shoots. And the last words from Gandhi's lips were, "Raam! Raam!" the name of God as he had remembered it all his life. Nothing else, not "oh," or "ooh," but "Raam! Raam!" This is the end of a life which was dedicated to absolute unselfish service and discipline. So there was no other cry of pain; his cry of pain was the name of God. This is within everybody's reach.

Whatever desire a human being holds very dearly during his lifetime, that very desire spearing the mind, dwells in the subtle body and goes to the next life. When the subtle body is again enwrapped with the gross body in rebirth, the seeds of desire spring up again and direct our human action. It seems as though our senses are running full force toward certain objects, not merely to lead a happy life here, but to establish a long-range karmic plan that would extend through many lifetimes. We are advised to observe, discipline and direct our thoughts, words and actions.

We quote here from the Garuda-Purana, Part 2, Chapter 13, verses 5-16:

> It is said in the Vedas that beings should live 100 years
> But die earlier only through the force of wrong action.
> He who does not study the scriptures

Does not follow the traditions of one's family out of laziness,
Abandons right actions and performs evil deeds.
Eats here and there
In one's own and every home without discipline
Loves another's wife or husband
Such action easily diminishes the lifespan.
One who has no faith, is impure and
Performs no japa, does not observe auspicious acts and signs,
A priest who imbibes intoxicants,
Goes under the rule of Yama.
The king who does not protect and follow the rule of law,
Is cruel, engaged in useless habits—
And such other acts of transgressions of one's duties
Lead him to come under the grip of death.
Daily ablutions, charity, japa,
Fire offerings, self-study, worship of God
The day these are not performed, that day has been lived in vain.
Knowing that the body goes so easily, O Lord of Birds,
And seeing the bondage of one's action,
Human beings should engage themselves in burning the residues of transgressions and sins.

And again:

Lord Krishna said:
As in a herd of a thousand cows,
A calf finds his own mother—
So the action performed in a previous life
Finds its doer in this life.

—Ch. 31, vs. 1

Excessive pride, too much speaking, not renouncing, anger, exclusive concern over one's own livelihood, betraying friends—these are the six sharp swords that cut down the lifespan; it is not death that kills human beings.

—Mahabharata, Udyoga-parvan 37. 10-11

It is the psychological effects of negative emotions,

attitudes and actions that cause the physiological imbalances which sap one's vitality, create warps in the energy fields of the body and thus produce all manner of illnesses. Finally the body can cope no more with such destructive acts, the karma catches up with time and death occurs.

These are not views simply held by theological texts but all the ancient Sanskrit works of medical science starting from *Charaka-samhita* have filled many chapters explaining that for phenomena of disease and death only the human wrong thoughts are responsible.

It is said that a soul may be born in a family to pay or receive a debt such as: (1) to recover a property that was held in trust and not returned, (2) to recover a debt, (3) to take revenge, or to pay back harm in return for the harm, (4) to serve in return for the service received, (5) to pay back a debt, (6) to be beneficial now to those who were beneficial before, and, finally (7) simply because in this family alone one's due of pain and pleasure in terms of karma as well as one's spiritual destiny would be fulfilled. On the other hand,

> Compassion towards the living beings; good works; meritorious deeds for a better after life; truth; speaking only to benefit other living beings; faith in the scripture (Vedas); honoring the guru, the celestial sages and adept sages; keeping company of the noble; . . . these are the marks of the pure souls who have returned from heaven to incarnate on earth.
> —Markandeya-purana XV, 42-44

Why do some people remember their previous lives while most of us do not? Every child is born with a vague memory of the past life but the emotional entanglements of this world overshadow the buddhi and that mirror is befogged again. It is just as well. Are not the woes of one lifetime a sufficient burden to carry then that we should try to remember the griefs and frustrations of many previous lifetimes? The oblivion is a process of starting with a clean slate again. The *jatismaras*, those who do continue to remember their previous lives have a certain predominance of *sattva*, purer aspect of nature, in their buddhi, and are therefore not disturbed by the memories, nor unduly attached to them. In the yoga tradition there are special mantras and other practices which by undertaking in this life, one may carry its memories, including the knowledge of sciences, into the next life. Similarly, by certain other practices such as concentration on *samskaras*, as taught by Patanjali, one may refresh the memory of previous lifetimes.

In order to establish the predominance of the purity of *sattva* in one's attitudes and resulting actions is essential. Through this purity alone one conquers the fear of death. For example, one of the most important ways to conquer the fear of death is the attitude of compassion, and compassionate acts, not merely towards human beings but towards all living creatures. One who realizes the unity of self, one life-force, one consciousness, as manifest in all life, masters the fear of death:

> He who sees all beings in self alone
> and sees self in all beings,
> thereafter has no more aversions.
> The wise man in whom all beings have become
> (his own) self,
> and he sees all oneness, thereafter
> Whence attachment, whence grief now?
>   —Isha Upanishad 6, 7

With this view many monks of the swami orders walk habitually with their eyes cast on the ground, and the

Jaina monks walk brushing the ground before them with a velvet brush, so that no living being may be crushed under their feet. A person of pure, sattvic perspective sees that the fear of death a cow experiences in a slaughterhouse is the same as a sick patient experiences in a hospital. A spiritually aspiring person does not wish to take on the karma of being the cause of any creature's death, as far as he can help it.

In the more advanced stages of karmic purity one must be cautious even in the practice of compassion and other good deeds so as to avoid physical attachments. Often a strong attachment may pull a very pure soul to a lower existence. The story is told in the Puranas of a rishi who opened his eyes from *samadhi* to see that a wounded doe, being pursued by a hunter, died, giving birth to a fawn in the process. The rishi's compassion moved him so that he neglected his meditation as he became totally engrossed only in the care of the fawn. The result was that the rishi himself was reborn as a deer for a time before subsequently regaining human life. However, in that life he became the famous Jada-Bharata, the fully enlightened sage.

The life force in the fawn and in the sage who is a candidate for enlightenment is one and the same. At the level of a beginner such knowledge of unity leads not merely to the practice of non-violence—to cause death to none—but even emotion is raised to a compassionate level. We hear in the folksongs of India how a dying doe addresses a hunter:

> Take all my flesh, hunter, leaving but the breasts
> And do let me go, please I beseech you;

> My little fawns who do not yet know to graze tender
>   grass,
> await looking to the path on which I may return.

It was for this reason that in the ancient Indian ashrams, all killing of beings was forbidden and the King must leave his bow and arrow outside the periphery of the ashram forest. We read in the words of Kalidasa, the ancient Sanskrit poet of the fourth century:

> Here in the ashram the animals are meek
> for they are not threatened by bondage or death.
> > —Raghu-vamsha 13.50

King Dilipa offers his own body to a lion in the forest who is ready to devour the ashram cow, Mandini. Says he,

> Having lived in solitude and having gained some
>   wisdom
> I can no longer have much faith in attachment toward
>   this body
> that is made merely of the five elements.
> > —Raghu-vamsha 2.57 by Kalidasa

In the beginning of his text, Kalidasa says,

> I shall sing of them who were pure throughout life,
> performed actions till the attainment of a goal,
> whose empire extended to the oceans,
> whose chariots made paths up to heaven,
> who offered their fire sacrifices in proper manner,
> fulfilled the desires of all who came to seek aught,
> punished only according to the intensity of the
>   crime,
> who awoke always in time,
> who gathered wealth in order only to give,
> whose words were measured to speak truth
> (so no untruth may slip from the lips),
> who gained glory but for their subjects
> who would give away their entire households,
> who practiced wisdom and learning in childhood,
> enjoyed the world in youth;
> in old age lived as renunciates and at the end,
> abandoned their bodies by the right processes of yoga.
> > —1.5-8 Raghu-vamsha by Kalidasa

Once again it is made clear that to die according to the processes of yoga one has to lead a life of purity, dedication and discipline. This path is not open to the licentious.

Kalidasa is, of course, speaking of a solar dynasty of kings, children of the Sun, their lineage running through the great Manu, the first man, who was the anthropomorphic incarnation of the cosmic principle called the *mantra*, and in whose honor all the Sanskrit texts teaching mantras and their application refer to any mantra as a "manu," which is related to the English word "man." All the kings of this dynasty, to which even the present day kings of India and of the Himalayan states trace their ancestry, were initiated by the family guru named Vasishtha into the solar science branch of yoga. The sage Vasishtha was their teacher for a hundred generations: he is the anthropomorphic incarnation of the prana principle: *prano vai vasishtha rsih.* Those kings initiated in the solar science thus became *maryada-purushas*, those who laid down the social and ethical traditions of the Indian society and whose behavior served as a model for the entire society for many thousand years. Kalidasa's eulogy thus is not a single praise but a statement of ideal life that culminates in ideal death. Solon the Greek would agree.

Only the philosophy of life described in verses 5-8 can give one such mastery over death. The compound phrase *tanu-tyaj*, to "renounce, abandon, leave, give up the body itself" is a key to that philosophy. Contrast it with the Western phrase "giving up the ghost." In the West we hear "I have a soul." In the Gita, we read of the soul who has the body. When we say, "I have a soul" who says it? The body that has no consciousness of its own? Is it the body that by its own volition decides to give up its ghost which is as it were, its possession? Kalidasa, in contrast, speaks of the masterful souls who knew otherwise, who by their volition renounced mentally and then gave up the bodies. For this, a pure life culminating in a renounced fourth state of life is a prerequisite. Is this what Dante means when he says:

> Then, in life's fourth division, at the last
> She weds with God again,
> contemplating the end she shall attain
> And looketh back . . .
> —Transl. Henry Francis Cary

TRANSITIONS

Much is read these days concerning out-of-body experiences. Those who have such experiences may often be humble and modest about it or puzzled by it. Others feel that they have perhaps the power of astral travel or have become great masters themselves! Nothing can be farther from the truth. An average body-bound person does not know much about the existence of *samashti-citta*, the collective unconscious of the universe. The word collective is somewhat misleading because it is not a collection of the individual minds put together. The individual minds are simply dots, like lightbulbs, in the common unconscious from which they derive much of their faculty. The word unconscious is also misleading. It is not that the mind is unconscious but that the individual mind is not conscious of this vast field which links us all, not only with each other in the present, but in this universal common mind is hidden the impressions of all the past and potentialities of the future of all the universes including the smallest possible individual event that might take place. By accident, sometimes, when the conscious mind is at rest or relaxed our awareness touches the edges of the unconscious where distant times and spaces are not distant. The sense of movement is false. It occurs because of our own frame of reference in which we reach distances only through physical movement. Therefore, we ascribe this accidental touch to the fringes of infinity in terms of a movement as though something came out of the physical body and traveled elsewhere. Shankaracharya says:

> Some say that the soul rises through the central channel leading to the head and then goes to higher realities through the solar paths, etc. That is incorrect because going implies a limitation in space, time, causation and fruition. Such false implication of space, time, causation and fruition, etc. cannot apply to the one who is firm in the true reality . . .
> —Commentary on Chandogya Upanishad 16.15 1-2

The reported feeling as though a silver chord was attached to the migrating astral body, like an umbilical chord, from the fontanelle simply indicates an accidental entry into the consciousness of the *sushumna* channel, again interpreted in terms familiar to our conscious and subconscious minds.

Such out-of-body experiences occur accidentally to the common persons for many reasons. There may be a strong unfulfilled desire, seeking out its objects. There may be a very strong karmic causation involved, forcing through the barriers. There may be a bond of relationship as in the case of a mother observing a son's accident from the distance. Or, the person may have had some yoga training in a previous life and is now ready for further instruction. In the last case he should maintain an attitude of purity and humility and seek out a perfect guide who may teach him to control the mechanisms which are hidden in the systems within the personality.

Does a soul after death go to heaven or hell, or does it reincarnate? On the surface it would appear to be a controversial question but it really is not, once the definition of heaven and hell is better understood.

There is also the question about the transition period. How long does one stay in heaven, hell or in the purgatory? How long does it take for one to reincarnate? Different cultures and traditions ascribe different time periods. It should be understood that the question of such temporality is irrelevant to the soul which is not limited to our sense of time. The sense of time for different states and levels of consciousness differs. For example, we must measure our time during a dream in two ways. The time an event seemed to take during the dream is quite real while the dream lasts. Yet it is not to be measured against a clock ticking in the same room where the dreaming person lies in bed. One might be tempted to suggest that, well, of course, the time being told by the clock is real; the time experienced during sleep is merely subjective. Such an assertion is based on the unproved assumption that what is subjective is unreal, which is not the case. Are our unexpressed mental thoughts, memories, feelings unreal?

Excepting the liberated Masters, all the experiences of a soul in transition from death through heaven or hell or a reincarnation occur within the subtle body. Our subtle body is constituted of a very refined level of material energies, such as pranas, powers of the senses and so forth, and serves as an individualized instrument of the universal unconscious. This individualized *chitta* serves as the repository of all our impressions which become the *samskaras*, creating latent tendencies which finally mature into karmic fruition. Some karma ripens at a physical level but some only on the mental level and within the subtle body. Just as our mental sicknesses—including milder disturbances—are part of the karmic fruition, so also are the experiences between death and the next life. It is important to note that the philosophical systems of India, including Buddhism, accept reincarnation as well as heaven and hell. The deeper aspects of the teaching make it clear that heaven and hell exist only in the subtle world. A number of passages in the Brhadaranyaka Upanishad (4.3.8-20) state that the experiences between death and rebirth are in the same category as dreams, a twilight zone. The wakefulness is like being in this body, in this world; the sleep and dream states are as though a transition after death and before rebirth. The life force, the soul wrapped up in the subtle body, sees whatever it has stored in its unconscious *chitta* and from its own light creates its own worlds, within its own time zone. The experiences of this zone of awareness draw from the previous life, the previous series of experiences and their samskaras.

According to the same Upanishad (4.4.6),

> . . . to whatever one is attached, he goes to that as a result of his actions, to whatever his subtle body and the mind are affixed. Coming to the end of that action whichever he has performed here, from that world he returns again to this world to perform

actions. Such is the state of those who desire . . .

This is the basis of the philosophy of the *Tibetan Book of the Dead*. Unfortunately the Tibetan Book seems to be written in a highly stylized symbolic and ritualistic language, often serving only as a breviary. The introductory essays to both translations available are a help in unravelling its mysteries. But more than these, only someone with a direct experience of initiatory death, like that of Nachiketas, can really interpret this work. In the words of H. H. Swami Rama, "What can a ritual do?" The theme of the Tibetan Book is centered around the fact of a secret power the true Guru has to lead a soul through the journey. The same view is held among the Sufis.

> In the fourth, and last, Journey, the Perfect Man guides others in their transition from what is generally considered to be physical death, to a further stage of development which is invisible to the ordinary person. For the dervish, therefore, the apparent break which takes place at conventional physical death does not exist. A continuous communication and interchange exists between him and the next form of life.
> —Indries Shah in *The Sufis*, p. 345

The transition from disincarnating to reincarnation has been divided in the Tibetan Book into three states called *Bardos*.

In the first part of the first Bardo a person is still inhabitating this body. The mind, however, begins to look to the other shore. The undercurrents of the subtle body begin to take on a greater reality. At this point:

> those who have not prepared themselves spiritually suffer much anguish, and should be helped with japam, spiritual practices and advice. They will go on the normal karmic path.

those who have prepared themselves are led by the
Guru.
The Guru joins his own consciousness to theirs and
death becomes a spiritual, transcendental experience.
They are also guided by the Guru to an appropri-
ately high birth;
those who are well advanced may be led by the
Guru's consciousness into final liberation.

At the time of the separation of the body and spirit, one
who is not yet liberated enters into experiences projected
from the subtle body, yet on the screen of the subtle body.
On this screen one may see that he is meeting Christ,
Krishna, Buddha or other guides. The experiences of those
mentioned by Dr. Moody in *Life After Life*, and by other
authors in similar contemporary publications, end at this
point. The unconscious mind takes over and one's samskaras produce an inner world. Having touched the fringes
of this inner world, one may even return to the world
without because his karmic duties toward others are not
yet complete. Death becomes a lesson and a guide. Having
seen its face once, the subject is no longer afraid of it.

If, however, the Bardo continues, a series of experiences unfolds. One may see benign deities, or ferocious
beings. Dr. Moody's Christian subjects saw Christ—but a
Jew would have an entirely different experience. The
subjects whom Karlis Osis and Erlunder Haraldsson studied
in India often saw divine figures from within the traditions of India. A Tibetan may see some of the figures
described in and expected from his tradition. Again,
depending on the contents of one's own mind, one may
see dead ancestors, guardian angels, or infernal figures of
some kind. One may go to heaven or hell, in a constantly
changing scenario.

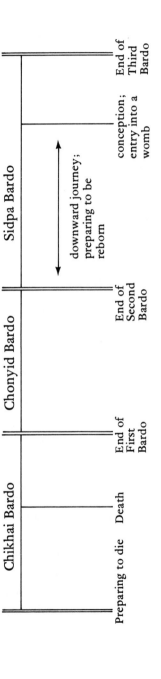

One's own faith in God, one's own prayer, mantram, is the only protection. The Tibetan Book speaks of bearing one's *yidam* in mind. A *yidam* is the spiritual focus of the mantra and the manifest symbolic forms that living energies take.

Persons with different levels of purity attained in the subtle body are tuned to corresponding *yidam* who, as it were, present him/herself at the person's unconscious invitation. These experiences are quite real to the person who has lost the physical body and must depend entirely on the feedback derived from the subtle body alone. To those who are purer of inner character an unseen divine hand guides through these karmic experiences. Those who have gone through higher yoga initiations in a previous life may even remember their mantram, which will bring forth its spiritual energy, *yidam*, for a guide.

If the karmic residue is little, one may attain final liberation at this point and shed his subtle body also. He says:

> Go, Death, to thine own path—
> Other than of the divine beings.
> —Yajur Veda 35. 7

If, however, the karmic residue is strong, the personality goes through a long period of the second bardo. Anguish of hell and pleasures of heaven seem to take on a more solid reality. One may see himself pass by a seat of judgment; or see himself in states of embodiments through 8,400,000 species—all or a few of them; through endless cycles of births and deaths for many eons or a few. The screen on which all these images play seems like a three-dimensioned world. For how long? Who knows? Who can judge the true duration of time in a dream. It is also possible that the entire second Bardo may be a long night of darkness, sleep which has resulted from much *tamasic* karma.

Gradually, as this aspect of the karma is exhausted, the subtle body begins to prepare for reincarnation. Somewhere in the world of limited space and time, on some planet, in some year or month, a couple or a family are waiting for the fruition of their karma through the addition of another person whose own karma must be added to the family's pool for perfect maturation. The subtle body of the disincarnate being is drawn per force toward this new space-time-causation coordinate. The third Bardo begins. The subtle body now produces a new series of images. These are images not from the past but from the future home. The sexual fantasies become a very strong part of these images. It is but appropriately so. Let us look at it this way.:

The strongest duality and dependence in our life is derived from the love of continuity of the body. The fear of death is another word for the same. As an antidote to this fear, we develop the urge to *praja*, progeny, through sexuality and reproduction. Death and sexuality are the two complementary poles of the same magnet that draws us into the cycle of karma and its fruition. So long as our attachment to the body remains, the sexual urge remains. The samskaras of this urge and of the body-attachment drag us down to reincarnation and repeated death, *punar-janman* and *punar-mrtyu*. So long as the slightest residue of the sex urge remains, the process of reincarnation cannot discontinue, the final spiritual liberation cannot occur. Total mental celibacy is the conquest of death, for then the flesh is no more an attraction or a hindrance.

According to the Tibetan Book the disincarnate person in the subtle body begins to see the visions of copulating couples. Finally the vision is centered on the copulating figures who are to be his parents. Their subtle bodies become attuned. The thoughts unite; conception occurs. But the Bardo is not yet over.

It takes the new personality a very long time to focus on the new baby, the new coordinates of space, time and dimensions. He is yet a creature of the two worlds. The visions of the past continue, both the memories and the subtle projections. We have already said elsewhere that no attempt should be made to draw his consciousness prematurely to our realm. At this time he remembers all his past incarnations:

> Foods of many kinds I have ingested,
> a variety of breasts suckled;
> oh, how many mothers I have seen—
> and fathers and friends.
> Now I lie upside down
> in this dark womb;
> But this time I shall search
> for the divine self.
> —Garbha Upanishad

> By the seventh month in the womb, a person remembers all sorrows, sicknesses, afflictions, old age, changes of form that have occurred in previous lives but when he comes out of the womb covered with the darkness of ignorance, he no longer remembers; becomes a child and in the youth is blinded with passion. He, however, who continues to see the reality finally attends liberation.
> —Garuda Purana, Part 2, Ch. 36, v. 20-22

Even though the fetus has no physical capacity for

such verbalized thought, the subtle body and the hidden mind are active. As the mind again begins to identify with the body, the subtle world is forgotten. The kundalini is again linked to the centers of psychophysiological functions, emitting into them just the minutest possible spark. This spark keeps the limited mind functioning, provides energy to prana, keeps the body alive and the personality remains bound to karma.

The compassion and grace of the Guru is infinite. When he has let a disciple take refuge in his spiritual bosom, he guides this disciple through many rounds of birth and death. How fortunate the disciple, yet how ungrateful, for whose liberation the Guru himself must be reborn. The Guru's guidance is not limited to the moments of death but also, now, on the shore to which the soul crosses over. The Guru often directs certain parents to prepare themselves to receive a certain soul. Oh, how fortunate the parents to whom such a guided soul is directed. By what process the Master recognizes a soul, we the uninitiated cannot know even though we read all about it in Patanjali's *Yoga Sutras* III. 53. At the appropriate time, the Master comes and again opens the kundalini of the reborn disciple who picks up his spiritual life at the chakra where he had left off in the last body.

A Master has abandoned all attachments to body, its karmas and their fruition. He adds nothing more to his subconscious mind. He has burnt all his samskaras in the fire of knowledge. He is now free of the previous dependence on the subtle body and dwells in the Superconscious. Such Masters constantly remind us:

> Like the spokes in the hub of a chariot,

That in whom all the channels are centered;
it is He who moves within, born manifold.
Meditate upon that Self thus: OM.
Fare ye well to go across (the channel of) darkness.

—Mundaka Upanishad 2.2.6

NOTES
CHAPTER 4

1. It is interesting to note that in the works like Dr. Moody's *Life After Life* the same theme occurs. When the persons experience leaving the body and encounter the "divine light" it commends them to return and continue in the same body because, and it is so in all the cases, they have yet to complete some act of service or love for someone else.

Immortality of the Masters

Let me relate to you the story of Siddhartha the Buddha—not the Herman Hesse story. Siddhartha was the birth name of Gotama the Buddha. At his birth the wise men had come and had prophesied that he would either be a great king, the emperor of the whole earth, or a great renunciate, an enlightened being. His father, the king, to ensure that his son not abandon his royal home and princely kingdom, not become an enlightened being, built a huge palace to wall the young boy from all unseemly, ugly sights of the world, so that the young prince should see no sickness, old age, or death, also so that he may not see an enlightened being either. He surrounded him with beautiful maidens and all kinds of luxuries. When the king thought that he was all absorbed and was enjoying himself and that there was no more danger of his becoming enlightened, he decided to take the young prince out in a royal procession to view the kingdom. After driving out for a little while, the prince saw a sick person.

"What is wrong with that man? Why are those people supporting him? Why does he not walk by himself?"

"Oh, he is sick."

"Sick? What does that mean?"

"Well, a sick person has something so wrong with his body that he has to have someone help him and support him."

"Does that happen often?"

His ministers answered, "Well, yes prince, it does. We have kept you sheltered away from all these things and kept you in good health, but yes, everybody gets sick sometime." Prince Siddhartha was so saddened by the revelation of this reality of life that he cut his procession short and returned to the palace grieving and pondering over the incident. Since there were wine and attractive damsels and all the usual luxuries to help him forget and when it seemed that this had happened, again his father ordered the prince to be taken in procession to see the rest of the kingdom. He sent word before to make sure that nothing unseemly would mar the sight of the prince and cause him grief. But as fortune would have it, after a little while Siddhartha saw an old man walking with a stick, with his back bent, hair all grey, with his skin wrinkled, no teeth, unable to stand without the support of the stick. Prince Siddhartha was surprised at this sight and questioned:

"What is that?"

"That is an old man."

"Old man?"

"Yes, an old man. That is the way people get after

many years of their life pass."

"Does that happen to everyone?"

"Sure it does, your highness."

"Will it happen to me too?"

"Surely it will, son."

Prince Siddhartha was even more saddened at this and again ordered the elephants to return to the palace. He had much to think about, to contemplate, to discuss with himself. Unfortunately nobody was allowed to answer his questions any more. The royal command went out that he was forbidden to such ideas and sights. They continued to surround him with all the pleasures of life and drown him with the love of all the maidens. Finally when the king again thought that his son had recovered from his previous sadness and experiences, he again had him out to view the sights of the kingdom, where he had made sure that no one sick or old was going to be out in the streets. After seeing all the beautiful gardens, flowers, and well built houses out of one of the small alleyways popped a small procession of four persons carrying a corpse on a bier on their shoulders. The astonished prince exclaimed, "What is that? Why are they carrying that man? Why does he not walk?"

"He is dead, sir."

"He is dead? What is that?"

"Why, Prince, you are so innocent. Do you not know? People get sick sometimes when they get old and then they die, and there is no life. They are going out of the city to the cremation ground and they will burn the body."

"Really? Does that happen to everybody?"

"Yes, of course."

"To me too, to this body? This well-decorated, handsome body? To all these youths, and attractive maidens? Are all their bodies going to be burnt in the cremation ground, and become ashes? This is indeed a tragedy. What kind of a life! Is that how all our lives will end?"

Again the prince had much to think about, much to contemplate and remarked, "Please turn the elephants back. I cannot bear to see all this, I do not understand it all. And no one explains anything to me."

When it seemed that he had outwardly forgotten all the unpleasant incidents he was again taken out this time surrounded by his ministers. The paths were all clear. Suddenly, "Please stop; who is that man?"

"Who?"

"That man there, the one with the shining face, wearing the bright orange robes like the color of the rising sun. He seems so happy in this world that is full of sickness, old age and death. He is smiling. Who is he? What is he?"

"Sir, he is a monk."

"Why does he wear those robes?"

"That is the garb of the renunciate, the monk. They wear the flowing robes colored with the tint of the rising sun."

"Why does he seem so happy?"

The Prince then expressed a desire to hold discourse with the monk to find out the secret of his happiness. Although everyone sees sickness, old age, death, and also those with the shining faces, yet everyone, unlike the Buddha, does not make use of the experiences to learn from. Gotama the Buddha was one of the very few, who one night calmly walked out of the luxuries and pleasures of the palace in search of that enlightenment that shone on the face of the monk. Buddha finally found the answers to the questions of sickness, old age and death.

Now here is another story much more recent in time, the nineteenth century. There was a great man named Swami Dayanand. I was born and brought up in the movement that he had established. There was a young man, well-versed in the Western sciences of the time who would come to argue with him about the existence of God. This young man, Gurudatt, would question and argue with the Swami day after day but finally one day he said: "Swami, you have closed my mouth with your arguments. I have no more questions, but still somehow, I cannot accept the existence of eternal life and of God. I do not feel the faith in me."

The Swami answered, "That is not for me to give. That is God's own gift of grace to give to you someday." Swami Dayanand was a great reformer. He has been compared in India to Martin Luther. He was responsible for getting rid of a lot of superstition and prejudices of his time in the society there. He was a being of great spiritual strength, but because of his outspoken behavior many attempts were made on his life whenever he said or did something that displeased someone. But because of his yoga accomplishments and fearlessness he managed to thwart the attempts. However, the last attempt involved his very own servant, the cook, who was heavily bribed to poison his meals. He was this time unable to expel all the tiny pieces of crushed glass that were mixed with his food and realized that the time had come for him to leave his body. The word went out that the swami was going. It was a special day in India, when we celebrate the Festival of Lights. The Swami took a bath as is the custom, sat in the lotus posture and told everyone to leave the room. However, the young argumentative Gurudatt hid behind a window curtain and witnessed the entire scene of the swami preparing for his death in such a careful but casual manner. He saw the swami sit and recite the sound of OMMMMM three times, saw him laugh, then smile, take a deep breath, expel it and die.

From that moment on Gurudatt had no more arguments, no more questions or doubts.

One of the books we usually recommend for reading is Gurudev Swami Rama's *Life Here and Hereafter* based on the Katha Upanishad. In this book is found a story that is very old, but very meaningful if properly understood. A long time ago there was a young man named Nachiketas, a brahmacharin, one who walks in God, an absolute celibate. As a young man, he saw his father performing a sacrifice which a pious man sometimes does, of giving everything away. His father, who actually was quite a hypocrite, announced this act of his, but instead of giving away all his possessions he only parted with those that were absolutely useless to him or to anyone—the cows which had already given all the milk they could. His son, recognizing the irony of the situation, said to him, "Father all that is yours you are giving away. To whom are you going to give me?" His father only quieted his son, but the latter being very persistent kept on with the question until his father frustratingly answered, "I will give you to Death."

Nachiketas went to the door of death—Yama, the god of death. However, Yama, a very busy being, was not at home, so Nachiketas patiently waited for him to return. For three days and three nights he lay at the door of death. Allegorically, when the high yoga initiations take place and a great master has touched his consciousness to yours you lie at the door of death, so to speak; you do not know whether you are in this body or not. Consciousness is all there but it seems as if the body is not there. You think you are speaking but you do not know whether you are actually speaking or not. Others hear only a single word whereas from your consciousness you have given a whole speech. Everything in the consciousness is internalized. Quite often the initiate may see his body lying there dead. He is puzzled over it. What is this? Why am I here? What is that?

But back to the door of death where Nachiketas is waiting: Yama finally returned and was horrified to see such piety and patience. A handsome holy youth lying at his door awaiting his return. He could not believe it, because Death is afraid of such powerful brahmacharins who come of their own accord to his door. This stems from a very basic principle of nature. Whatever you treasure most, you love most, desire most in life, and would like to have, would like to keep, you turn away from it a little, surrender it a little and it will remain yours. On the opposite hand, whatever you detest most in life, absolutely dislike, just turn to it a little, and it will stay away from you. It is the principle of innoculation. It applies to all sciences. Poison is cured by poison. Everything is its own antidote. So life has death built into it.

The only way to master death is not to run away from it, but to turn to it a little, recognize it daily. We must fully understand the relationship of rebirth with death. In the current usage as well as in the great theological texts of India there occurs a word *punar-janman*, being born again, rebirth. Another word is *punar-bhava*, to come into the worldly cycle again. But in the most ancient texts from the earliest times to approximately 1,000 B.C., the term used is not rebirth but *punar-mrtyu*, to die again. The prayers in these texts are not for freedom from reincarnation but for freedom from dying again and again. It is the freedom from repeated death, presumably from reincarnation, that Nachiketas seeks in the Katha Upanishad (eighth century B.C.). Here we summarize the story of Nachiketas from the text much older than the Katha Upanishad. The text is Taittiriya Brahmana, the date of which is lost in antiquity. The text being translated here for the first time, devotes the entire eleventh section of the third book to kindling the ritual fires named *Nachiketasa* or *Nachiketa*, the term that commemorates the fact that Nachiketas received this knowledge from Yama, the god of Death. The story of Nachiketas occurs here in the following brief version. We quote it here for the benefit of those who have not yet read the detailed version as it occurs in the Katha Upanishad where the entire metaphysical teaching about the immortal nature of the universal spirit has been taught by Death to the young ascetic. The version offered here is presented according to the commentary of Sayana, the greatest commentator ever born, a wise man and Prime Minister of the Vijayanagar Empire of the thirteenth century A.D.:

> The sage Uddalaka, born in the family of the sages
> of Gotama lineage, known for his great gifts of grain
> once decided to perform the sacrifice of giving all his
> belongings. He had a son named Nachiketas. As he
> was a young man a great feeling of devotion entered
> his mind, thinking, "My father is giving everything
> that is his, to whom should he give me?" He repeated
> the question a second time and again a third time.
> The father thought, "He is not dumb, he's only
> making trouble." Angry, he said to the son, "I give
> you to Death!"

As the boy got up to go away from near his father,
an Invisible Voice spoke to him and said, "Young
man of the Gotama lineage, your father has said, "Go
to the house of Death. I have given you to Death so
you should go to the house of Death but only when
Death is visiting away from his home. When you
arrive there, stay without food for three nights.
When Death, returning, asks you how many nights
you were there, tell him "three."

Death will ask: "What did you eat the first night?"
Say, "I ate up your progeny."

"What did you eat the second night?"
Say, "I devoured all your wealth (cattle and so
forth)."

"What did you eat the third night?"
Say, "All your good deeds."

The boy did exactly as he was advised by the
Invisible Voice, meaning that through this act of in-
hospitality of not offering food and drink to a wise
man who had come as an uninvited guiest, Death has
been cursed with the loss of progeny and wealth and
all the results of his good deeds such as happiness of
good karma and spiritual advancement!

"I pay homage to you, my Lord," said Death.
"Please ask for a grant of boons to make up for my
infringement of the rules of honoring someone such
as yourself." The first boon Nachiketas asked: May I
return to my father alive.

Second boon he asked: May my good deeds of
both kinds—ceremonials and rituals as well as acts of

charity and compassion—become inexhaustible. In response to this second request, Death taught Nachiketas the fire rituals. He who understands this Nachiketa fire, his good deeds of both kinds are never exhausted, that is, they continue to bear fruit. Death said, "Ask me for the third boon." Nachiketas said, "Teach me the way to conquer and banish *panar-mrtyu*, the return to death again." Death taught him of another fire whereby he conquered and banished the repeated death. He who thus kindles the Nachiketa fire conquers and banishes repeated death—so does he who understands it fully.

—Taittiriya Brahmana III. 11.8

There are two ways of kindling fire, says Sayana, the way of the external fire and the way of the fire of inner sacrifice and internal worship. This is made clear in the following passages of the text:

Lord, the Progenitor, undertook great asceticism. He poured an offering of gold into the fire-offering repeatedly but his wish was not fulfilled. Then he poured the gold offering into the universal fire that dwells in the heart, the very Self, and only then was his wish fulfilled. —(TB. III. 11.8)

He who has found the inner golden treasure which is immortal and pours this treasure into the fire of the Spirit, has learned that art which fully conquers repeated death and reincarnation. The yogis know of this gold and of this fire, and are made resplendent in its brilliance, even when they are abandoning the physical body through their own volition. The message inherent in this story, among others, is evident and repeated in the scriptural traditions of the whole world: in order to conquer death, one must pass through death. It is interesting that during the forty-nine days' fast before the final enlightenment, Buddha is faced by Mara, a term analogus to *mrtyu* (death) who, like the god of death in the Nachiketas story of Katha Upanishad, tempts Buddha with offers of worldly empire, beautiful maidens, everlasting luxuries and so forth. So also is Jesus tempted by Satan at the end of the forty days' fast in the desert. It is, however, important to remember that in the Nachiketas story as in the entire tradition of Indian and yoga philosophy, death is not a force of evil. The god of death is Yama, the son of Sun, *Vivasvat*, the keeper of karma and karmic time. In the story of Savitri and Satyavan referred to elsewhere, Yama pleads innocent of the charge of cruelty for he himself is also bound by the universal laws of karma. To conquer death is not to conquer evil, only to give right direction to one's karma in order to conquer the process of repeated death and reincarnation.

To enter the house of death one needs a guide as is evident in the Nachiketas story as well as in Dante's *Inferno*.

The disciple is required to have a guide, a teacher who has been through the gates of death before. In Dante's work, Virgil had been there and in the Katha Upanishad, the Lord of Death himself. There are rare ones born once in a thousand years perhaps who have traveled through the gates of death unguided as did Ramana Maharshi, of whom we speak elsewhere. Otherwise the guidance of a qualified Guru who himself has mastered the art of death is absolutely necessary to understand the processes of death by personal experience and come back unscathed by the fire of the inferno.

It is regrettable that not much attention is paid to Dante's *Paradiso* which sings of the Transcendental beyond death. Dante crosses through the infernal death but in

Paradise sees the universal form of the Lord, as did Arjuna
see *Virat* or *Vishva-rupa* in the tenth and eleventh chapters
of the Bhagavad-Gita. At the end of his work, Dante recalls
his vision:

> O eternal beam!
> (Whose height what reach of mortal thought may
>   soar?)
> Yield me again some little particle
> Of what thou then appearedst . . .
> O grace, unenvying of thy boon! that gavest
> Boldness to fix so earnestly my ken
> On the everlasting splendor, that I look'd
> While sight was unconsumed; and, in that depth,
> Saw in one volume clasp'd of love, what'er
> The universe unfolds; all properties
> Of substance and of accident, beheld,
> Compounded, yet one individual light
> The Whole. And of such bond methinks I saw
> The universal form; for that whene'er
> I do but speak of it, my soul dilates
> Beyond her proper self; and, till I speak,
> One moment seems a longer lethargy,
> Than five-and-twenty ages and appear'd
> To that emprise, that first made Neptune wonder
> At argo's shadow darkening on his flood . . .
> O eternal light!
> Sole in thyself that dwell'st; and of thyself
> Sole understood, past, present, or to come . . .
>   —Paradise, tr. by Henry Francis Cary[1]

In the Bhagavad-Gita, Lord Krishna says to Arjuna:

> As the waters of different rivers enter the ocean,
> which though full on all sides remains undisturbed,
> likewise he in whom all enjoyments merge themselves
> attains peace; not he who craves after such enjoy-
> ments. He who gives up all desires and moves free
> from attachments attains peace, Arjuna. Such is the
> state of the God-realized soul. Having reached this
> state, he overcomes delusion and, established in this
> state even in the last moment he attains the bliss of
> God, even at the last moment.

Also Christ said die and then you will be born! but today the real meaning of his words has been lost. He was speaking in terms only understood in the deepest mystic traditions of the world.

Refer again to the Gita where Krishna says . . . as a man takes off old garments and puts on new ones, so does this embodied soul change its bodies and reincarnates. A full realization of this, a knowledge that this physical body is only the shell that houses the soul takes away the fear of death. The questions that we refuse to ask when we are alive, well, passionate and youthful those very questions present themselves at the time of death. The more we avoid the questions during a happy and healthy life, the more difficult it becomes to overcome the sense of puzzlement and confusion at the hour of death. Start asking yourself those questions now, while there is still youth, while the body is healthy, while the eyes sparkle and the teeth still gleem. While the skin is not wrinkled and the back is not bent; begin to inquire into death, for death is what you fear and are most averse to. Start asking now, go a little towards it.

There is a story of a seventeen-year-old revolutionary during the time that India was fighting against the British. This body was caught for anti-British activities and brought before the court. The judge said that he would be charged for treason and sentenced to death. However, in view of his early age he could take life imprisonment instead, if he would only apologize. The youth's reply was that he would rather die, for, if he was to go to prison he would have to spend untold years there wasting time, while if he were hanged, he would obtain a new body in a short while and return again, and as a youth be able once more to fight for his mother country. The question of faith and belief here is important.

There is a verse often quoted in India:

When you were born you cried
And the whole world rejoiced.
Live such a life that when you die
The whole world cries and you rejoice.

A Master rejoices at his reunion with God in death while the seekers cry.

There was a great saintly yogi master in India who died in 1950, by the name of Raman Maharshi, a man of great wisdom and realization. On Thursday, April 13th, a doctor brought him a palliative to relieve the congestion in the lungs but he refused it. "It is not necessary. Everything will come right in two days," he said. At about sunset he told the attendants to sit him up. They knew already that every movement, every touch was painful. But he told them not to worry. He sat with one of the attendants supporting his head. A doctor began to give him oxygen but was motioned away with a wave of the right hand. Unexpectedly, a group of devotees sitting in the veranda outside the hall began singing a hymn. On hearing it the yogi's eyes opened. He gave a brief smile of indescribable tenderness. From the outer edges of his eyes a tear of bliss and joy rolled down upon hearing the hymn. He took one more deep breath, and no more. No struggle, no spasms, no outer sign of death. He took one breath, only the next breath did not come.

—Philip Kapleau in *Wheel of Death*

The idea of death as something frightening is well known to all of us. But the idea of death as neutral, as something that doesn't matter, is not known. One is reminded of stories and great works of mythology and philosophy. In the Indian philosophy for example, is found the story of a man, a sage named Dadhichi. It was felt in a cosmic war between the forces of good and evil, devas and asuras, that the only weapon that would defeat the forces of evil, would be one built out of the bones of a man who would give them for this purpose out of an absolutely unselfish attitude. This great sage had sat in *samadhi*, in eternal meditation, for a thousand years. Knowing in his meditation what was passing on the cosmic scale he opened his eyes and offered to the gods his own bones. He shed his flesh and his bones were taken. The weapon, *vajra*, the thunderbolt of Indra, was built to defeat the evil in the cosmos. This *vajra*, known as *dorje* in Tibet, is the figurative weapon with which the yogis fight evil and death.

We have spoken earlier of the cycle in which death and birth unite at a single point. These cycles of individual life and death are mere mirror-reflections of the vast universal cycles, *kalpas*. The principle of universal causation becomes the individual karma. The causation becomes the flux of the cosmic time, *kala*, from Sanskrit, *kal*, " to calculate, to measure." *Kalah Kalayati bhutani*: Time calculates the existence of the beings. Time, according to the philosophy of Patanjali is but this:

> When some of the attributes latent in an entity manifest themselves, become active, they are said to be in the present.
> When these very attributes become unmanifest, dissolve to remain dormant within the entity, they are now said to be past, but they are still present as unmanifest.
> Other attributes that are lying dormant are yet to become manifest, active; they are in the future. They, too, are present as unmanifest.
> —Paraphrased from Vyasa *Commentary on the Yogasutra III. 12.*

In this vibrant flux nothing ever ceases to be. The vibration arises in the great Conscious Force, *cit-shakti*, whose name in this context is *maha-kali*, the great force ruling over time. Among her thousand names are Dissolver, Witness of the Great Dissolution, *maha-pralaya-sakshini*. She is the destroyer of time, *kala-hantri*, because she is herself free of birth and death: *anadi-nidhana*. She is the Beauty of the three worlds: *tripura-sundari*, and her power of the cycles of creation and dissolution is praised thus:

> Gathering the tiniest specks of dust from thy lotus feet Lord Brahma creates all these worlds.
> The great snake somehow bears them on a thousand heads, and Shiva, dissolving them, rubs their ashes on his limbs.
>
> —Saundarya-lahari vs. 2

When this *cit-shakti*, the vibrant power of cosmic and transcendental consciousness is realized, she comes true to her other names:

> *mrtyu-mathani*, she who crushes death.
> *jara-dhvantra-ravi-prabha*, the light of the sun on the darkness of old age and decay.
> *janma-mrtyu-jara-tapta-jana-vishranti-dayini*, she who gives rest to those who are suffering from birth, death and old age.
>
> —Lalita-sahasra-nama, verses 49, 143, 159

There is no way to describe her power fully:

> To honor the Sun, the Lord of days, with candle flames,
> To worship moon with dew from a moonstone
> To quench the ocean's thirst with ocean's own drops
> Such is my speech offered to thee in prayers and praises.

We are the candleflame, the moonstone's dew, the ocean drop. When our horizons expand, we are the Sun, the Moon, the Ocean. In this Sun, the flickering flames know no death. In this Moonlight the dewdrop is ever present.

In this Ocean, the drops dwell eternally.

A single compassionate glance of *cit-shakti*, the Mother of the Universe, a single vibration of her consciousness and creativity is said to equal 22,468,679,259,648, 000,000,000,000,000,000,000,000,000,000,000 human years, encompassing all the universes and whatever is contained therein. What is the force of a single creature's breath and brain power through an entire lifespan within this single vibration?

> The same one who is the night of our individual sleep
> is the night of the great Dissolution.
> The same shakti is the great maya of the universe.
> —Devi-mahatmya 11.22

This maya dwells in Brahman—the Transcendental It, whose spark constitutes the Self of all sentient beings. The conquest over death is nothing but the knowledge of the immortality of Self. Yajnavalkya was the greatest philosopher and wise man of his time, highly honored in the court of King Janaka who was himself a living master and a patron of philosophers and wise men. Yajnavalkya answered questions in the assemblies of philosophers that were held in Janaka's court—the questions no other philosopher could answer. At one point one of his answers so excited the wise king that he rose from his throne and said: "For this one sentence I give you a thousand cows with gold-studded horns!"

Thus Yajnavalkya had gathered much wealth that was in those days counted in cattle. Having provided enough for the upkeep of his family, he said to his wife: "Now I depart, Maitreyi."

"Where do you go?" Maitreyi asked.

"I go to attain *Amrta*, immortality of the Self.

There is enough here to provide for you."

She said, "Yajnavalkya, my husband, even if I were to inherit this entire earth full of wealth will I attain the knowledge of immortality?"

"No," said the great sage. "Yours will be the life of great comfort which comes to the well-provided, but there is no hope of immortality from wealth."

Maitreyi's reply is worth recording in gold letters. "What use have I for that which will not give me the knowledge of immortality? Then teach me all you know."

The dialogue continues with Yajnavalkya explaining the spiritual Self to be immortal, the only being worth pursuing in knowledge (Brhadaranyaka Upanishad 2.4.ff; 4.5ff).

mrtyor ma amrtam gamaya
Lead me from death to immortality:

—this is not a prayer for the survival of the body as is often the case in the Semetic view but a prayer for recognition, realization of the immortality of the spirit, the true Self, the life-force, the Consciousness-force.

One of the most important sections of the Mahabharata, the great epic, is the dialogue of Sanatsujata. Great teacher Vidura is teaching the king, Dhrtarashtra. Vidura advises that the king should seek further knowledge from Sanatsujata.

"How would I find that great sage?" asked the king.

"Simply close your eyes and think of him," says the teacher, upon which Sanatsujata appears.

The king, after offering appropriate honors, asks him, "Sanatsujata, I hear that you teach there is no such thing as death. Yet all the beings have been advised to

practice Brahmacharya for the conquest of death. Which
of these two beliefs should I then accept?"

Sanatsujata devotes four chapters discussing this
question and declares that:

> only ignorance and negligence are death.
> There is no such thing as death
> which might come like a tiger and devour a being.
> Who has ever seen a form called death?
>   —MB. Parvan 4, ch. 42, v. 5

Sanatsujata goes on to elucidate the nature of Self:

> I am your mother, I am your father as well as your
>   son.
> I am the Self of it all, all that is not and all that is.
> I am the old grandfather, the father and the son.
> You all are dwelling in my own Self. You are not
>   mine nor am I yours.
> Atman, the Self alone, is my dwelling; Self, my
>   birth.
> All-pervading I have an undecaying foundation.
> Unborn I move day and night without languor;
> knowing me, the wise man then dwells happy.
> Subtler than the subtle, of peaceful mind dwelling
>   in all beings,
> father of all beings, the wise man knows this Self
>   placed in the lotus.
>   —Mahabharata, parvan 4, ch. 46, v. 28-31

Shankaracharya, in his commentary on the above passage,
adds the following verses from his tradition:

> Ever-pure, ever-wise aspect the Lord—
> cultivating this One within the self.
> Withholding the six senses, unmoving,
> The reality is solid consciousness,
> the cause of the birth of the moving world.
> It is not the ever-vanishing world born of that con-
>   sciousness that removes darkness
> The one enunciator of That, the one world ever
>   immortal, never affected
> The witness of the vrittis of mind, Ever-Bliss, I am
>   That, I am That.

The yogi is not interested in the death of the body. His interest lies in freedom from the cycles of death and rebirth. This freedom is synonymous with the realization that the spirit neither dies nor is reborn. So we hear from an anonymous Sanskrit author:

> Why do you fear death?
> Would death spare someone afraid?
> Death cannot grab one who is not born.
> Then seek freedom from the process of rebirth.

According to Avadhuta-Gita, the song of the renunciate mendicant:

> Death or non-death is all negation;
> doing or non-doing is all negation.
> If everything is continuous, one, all Shiva,
> how does one speak of migrating, coming and going?
> —VI. 11

The sages of the Upanishads proclaim:

> As the sun, the eye of the whole world
> is not smeared with the faults of the beholder's eye
> so that One, the Inner Self of all beings
> is not smeared by the external sorrows of the
> common world.
> —Katha Upanishad 2. 2. 11

> This is that great unborn Atman without aging, without death.

> It is immortal, free of fear, for Brahman is without fear.

> He who knows thus becomes Brahman.
> —Brhadaranyaka Upanishad 4. 4. 25

> In whom the heaven, earth, and sky
> are interwoven as well as the mind with all the
> pranas—
> know that One alone as Self.
> Abandon all other speeches,
> this alone is the bridge of immortality.
> —Mundaka Upanishad 2. 25

This immortal being is the life-force permeating the whole universe. Here we paraphrase from the Shvetaketu narrative in the Chandogya Upanishad:

> Make a cut at the base of a tree, some sap flows.
> Make a cut in the middle of the tree, the same sap flows.
> Mat a cut at the topmost part of the tree, yet the same sap flows.
> It indicates the life-force present throughout the tree.
> The life-force leaves one branch, that branch withers and dies.
> The life-force leaves another branch, that branch withers and dies.
> The life-force leaves the entire tree, the tree withers and dies.
> Abandoned by the life-force the tree dies. It is not the life-force that dies.
> So is the whole universe permeated by one Life-force.
> It abandons (its operation in) one body, that body dies.
> It abandons (its operation in) another body, that body dies.
> The universal Life-force does not die.
> So it is. That universal Life-force is the Reality;
> That is the Truth;
> That is the self (atman).
> That self, O Shvetaketu, you are.
> Tat tvam asi: That thou art.
> —Chandogya Upanisahd 6. 11

"That thou art" is one of the four fundamental great sentences, *mahavakyas*, in the Vedanta doctrine, which itself is the end of all wisdom. *Cit-shakti*, the consciousness-force contracts and expands its *vrtti*, operation, in a given entity but She does not die. She ever dwells in *atman,* the Self. *Soham-asmi*: I am that Self—thus does a yogi and an aspirant after immortality always remember the nature of transcendental reality. Thus does he become immortal.

Again in the same narrative the father, Aruni, teaches his son, Shvetaketu:

> My pure child, a person is suffering from fever of illness. His kinsmen surround him as he is about to die and ask him, "Do you recognize me, your father, your son, your brother?" Only so long as his speech is not absorbed into prana, the prana into the Inner Light, the Light into the Supreme Deity, does he recognize them.
> But when his speech is dissolved into prana, prana into the Inner Light, the Inner Light into the Supreme Deity, he no longer recognizes them.

Shankaracharya's commentary says:

> This order of the dying process for a man of the world also applies for the enlightened one's attainment of the state of Reality. When the light has gone into the Supreme Self, he no longer recognizes (his kinsmen). The unenlightened leaves the Reality and enters a state of becoming an animal such as a tiger and so forth or a human or a celestial being. A wise enlightened one enters the Brahman-Self, the True Reality, which is shining to him through the candle of the light of knowledge born of the teaching of a great teacher. Some say that the soul rising through the central channel leading to the head then goes to higher realities through the solar paths, etc. That is incorrect because going implies a limitation in space, time, causation and fruition. Such false implication of space, time and causation and fruition, etc. cannot apply to the one who is firm in the True Reality and sees the oneness of the Real Self because that would be a contradiction. Any migration is inapplicable (in such a case) because ignorance, desires and actions which are the causes of such migration have been destroyed by the fire of true knowledge (in the case of such enlightened ones).
> —Chandogya Upanishad 6. 15

Again and again the ancient teachings equate immortality with the knowledge of the Spiritual Self:

> He who knows that Supreme Brahman becomes
> Brahman Itself;
> no one is born in his generations who would not
> know Brahman.
> He swims across grief, crosses over sin.
> Freed from the knots of the cave, he becomes im-
> mortal.
> —Mundaka Upanishad 3. 29

The knots of the cave are the blocks in the chakras. These blocks maintain our identification with the psycho-physiological functions. When the chakras are no longer "in knots," *cit-shakti* flows freely and the immortality of the spirit is realized. As *cit-shakti* flows freely and rises, the rishi declares:

> From the earth I rise to the skies;
> from the skies I rise to the heavens.
> From the heavens free of sorrows
> I reach the Light that is freedom.
> —Yajur-Veda 17. 67

> I know the great Person shining as the Sun beyond
> darkness.
> Only upon knowing Him one supercedes death.
> There is no other path for one to follow.
> —Yajur-Veda 31, 18

It is then that the yogi rises beyond the conquest of death. As he recognizes the immortality of Self, he no longer recognizes that there is such an experience as death. Dwelling in God, he no longer sees any time, space and causation that might conceivably be outside God's immortality. As we hear Milton say:

> Death over him, no power shall long usurp.
> —*Paradise Lost,* XII, 420-421

and again:

> Whence thou return'st and whither went'st I know;
> for God is also in sleep.
> —*Ibid.* XII, 610-611

He is no longer in search of Self-realization for he knows Self:

> Free from joy and sorrow,
> he neither dies nor does he live.
>   —Ashtavakra-Gita 18.83

The sage Markendeya sings:

> I have taken abode with the immutable Lord
> who manifests himself as bearer of conch and discus
> What can death do to me?
> I have taken refuge in him who is the soul of all beings;
> the great soul, the origin of sacrifice, born of no womb, the universe-form.
> What can death do to me?
>   —The song of Markandeya
>   Garuda-Purana 225. 2-6

This state of knowledge is open to all who seek. The Katha Upanishad ends with the statement:

> Nachiketas obtained this science and the entire method of yoga as taught by Death.
> Attaining Brahman he became free of all dust and rose above death;
> So also may anyone who knows this science of the Inner Self.
>   —2. 3. 18

NOTES
CHAPTER 5

1. International Collectors Library, Doubleday.

Conquest of Death

One cannot begin to understand the process of death and rebirth without full comprehension of the systems within the human personality with which the pure Self comes into a relationship of bondage. These major systems within the personality are:

The gross body, with all its anatomy, internal organs, nerves, muscles, the brain waves made up of the five gross elements.

The subtle body with its seventeen constituents (for detail see Swami Rama's *Lectures on Yoga*)

Four aspects of the inner sense *(antah-karana)*
Manas (active mind)
Buddhi (faculty of intelligence, discrimination and intuition)
Citta (the individual storehouse of all impressions, *samskaras* and *vasanas* including the faculty of subconscious mind)

Ahamkara (ego, the instrument of false identification between the pure self and the personality constituted of material elements)

Five *Koshas* (sheaths or veils around the pure Self)

Annamaya (made up of food; gross body)

Pranamaya (made up of *prana* with breath as the intermediate between the *annamaya* and *pranamaya*) and the five *pranas*:

Prana
Apana
Samana
Udana
Vyana

As well as five sub-pranas

Manomaya (sheath of mental processes)

Vijnanamaya (the sheath that establishes the identity of cognitive processes)

Anandamaya (the sheath that establishes the identity of pain-pleasure processes)

(These sheaths are the instruments of false identification.)

Causal body (karana-sharira)

(This is constituted of the first disequilibrium of *sattva*, *rajas* and *tamas*, the three gunas, the further disequilibrium of which produces the universe, the physical body and all mental processes.)

Kundalini (the ray of the divine Self, the source of our life and consciousness);

the three major channels of the *kundalini*:
ida, pingala and *sushumna;*

325,000 energy currents which are sent forth from the three major currents of the *kundalini*; seven *chakras*, the main centers of psychophysiological functioning which derive their power from the three-fold channel; innumerable other *chakras*, centers of psychophysiological functioning, distributed throughout the personality wherever any two of the 325,000 energy currents cross.

The yogi establishes full control over each and every one of these systems within the personality, by following disciplines, both of attitude and yoga practice, through many lifetimes. He begins with the practice of *yamas* and *niyamas* as taught in the Yoga-sutras of Patanjali. For the mastery over death he begins with the practice of *ahimsa*, nonviolence, *maitri* or Buddhist *Metta*, friendship toward all creatures; and *abhayam*, fearlessness which does not mean bravery but granting to all creatures that "I am no source of harm to any sentient being," "May no sentient beings fear me," "I shall not be a direct or indirect cause of harm or death to any living being." There are twenty-seven different levels of nonviolence that have been described by Patanjali. When a person is no longer the source of any cause of death for any sentient being, he has naturally established mastery over death. Such total mastery does not come by until all the systems within the personality have been penetrated, brought under the full control of the Consciousness Principle, the pure Self. Here we shall attempt to describe some of the disciplines that the yogi may undertake and master.

After the yogi has fully understood the consciousness of all sentient human beings by placing himself in the postures imitating these beings, and has understood the karmic processes involved in bringing oneself through many reincarnations in many bodies of many beings, the practice of hatha yoga has been accomplished. The practice of the corpse posture, *shava-asana* now begins. There are twenty-seven progressively intricate exercises of relaxation and concentrations that are performed in the corpse posture. The purpose of these exercises is to calm the conscious mind. As the conscious mind calms the physical body relaxes. The bondage of the neuromuscular system over the mind is loosened. The gross elements then no longer suppress the subtler elements from fully expressing their powers within the personality. In the state of *shava-asana* the yogi begins to understand what Patanjali has termed *prachara*, circulation. This means the pathways through which the sparks of consciousness circulate through the physical personality. The processes of *shava-asana* are like processions or circumambulations around a temple and through the corridors and vestibules of the same temple of God which is the human personality. Gradually the hidden niches and corners are found where little lights burn unseen.

Through the process of *shava-asana* practices the yogi enters the subtle body, leaving the physical body behind. This is important for the following reason: a soul in bondage of karma leaves behind the physical body through the process of death but carries with it the subtle body in which all the *samskaras* and *vasanas* are hidden. Freedom from the karmic process means the liberation from the *samskaras* and *vasanas*. The yogi who is free of the delimiting personal ego no longer requires the subtle body. Unlike the average person he leaves even the subtle body behind at the hour of death. This is what constitutes his mastery of the dying process. He may or may not decide to continue to utilize the causal body, depending on whether or not he wishes to return to the world to continue a mission through another life. Through the *shava-asana*, corpse posture, processes, functioning of the subtle body is understood, the five sheaths are penetrated, and entry into the connections which exist between the *chakras* and the psychophysiological operations is gained. Then the practices of *pranayama* are no longer simple physical processes of breath control but the *pranayama* sheath is awakened and penetrated.

When one learns to establish control over the breathing process, naturally, the cessation of breath, death, comes under control. Let us take, for example, the exercise of alternate nostril breathing, channel purification or *nadi-shodhana*. An average beginner cannot control the activity or passivity of the alternate nostril, but the yogi can switch on the activity of whichever nostril he wishes and performs his channel purification without the need to press the nostrils with his fingers. He does so because of his control over the subtle body, the *pranamaya* sheath, as well as the three-fold channel of *kundalini*. He can go into the depth of meditation and remain there for many hours or days with both nostrils flowing with equal strength. Such a person naturally has no regard whatsoever for sexual experience or for the death experience because in these two lower experiences the two nostrils flow with equal strength only for a brief moment as compared to the yogi's flow of the *sushumna* force unhindered and at the command of his will. About this requisite control of pranas in the yogi's dying process Shankaracharya states:

> This brahman is the same as the one who shines in the orb of the sun or in a person's right eye. Both of these are interdependent. That external sun is established in this person with its rays called the *pranas* and vice versa (for the *pranas* are the rays). When the enlightened being is about to rise (that is to die), he sees this orb in its purest form and (mere) rays no longer have to follow him.
> —Brhad-aranyaka Upanishad 5.5.2

Within the personality the location of the fifth *prana* is from the throat center up. When the yogi has mastered the lower *pranas, prana* and the *apana*, the ingoing energy flow and the outgoing energy flow, to such a degree that the two are wedded together, the inflowing and the outflowing no longer have this dichotomy of in and out. Then he acquires a natural cessation of breath known as *sahaja-kumbhaka* in which no effort is involved at the retention of breath. As consciousness is withdrawn from the body and autogenic controls become natural to the yogi the breathing process is naturally brought under such complete control. The next point is the mastery of the *udana prana.*

Udana prana is the *prana* controlling the dying process. When the entire life force is gathered into the head the *udana prana* helps it to migrate from there. Here the yogi learns to open his fontanelle, the place where the newborn babies have a soft spot. The yogi opens it at will. The yogi even uses this power of will when he is helping to die the liberated death; under the guru's touch the dying disciple's fontanelle may open.

Here we come to *yoga-nidra*, the yoga sleep. An average person asleep is not aware of his surroundings so we believe that sleep is outside the control of our free will, but Patanjali speaks of the attainment of *samadhi*, according to H. H. Swami Rama's unpublished commentary on the Yoga-sutras, by learning to observe sleep itself consciously. This conscious sleep was demonstrated by him in the Menninger Foundation experiment where the monitoring instruments indicated the presence of solid delta brain waves and yet he was able to repeat the sentences spoken softly in his presence. It is said in the scriptures

> *Pranagnaya evaitasmin pure jagrati*
> The prana fires remain burning in this city.
> —Prashna Upanishad 4. 3

In the light of those prana fires the free will remains active. It must be understood that the processes of wakefulness, dream and sleep occur only in the surface areas of the mind but there are vast extensions of the energy-field of the mind which are not affected at all by these three states of consciousness. Those areas of the mind remain active in the subtle body as well as remain in touch with *sakshin*, the Witness, the unobserved observer, the unsleeping, ever-wakeful, purest Self. Death has been often compared to sleep. He who masters the sleep process, so that he may consciously observe the sleeping parts of his mind, thereby masters also the dying process. The commentaries on the Yoga-sutras say: When we wake in the morning we often say, "I slept deeply"; who was keeping record of the depth of sleep? The answer is the ever-wakeful witness. It is the same wakeful witness who observes the dying process also.

This very witness principle is brought into our active daily life through the practice of mindfulness when we are taught ever to be mindful of our body posture, the state of our spine, the functioning of our internal organs, breath and all its states, the state of our emotions and thoughts almost instantly as they arise, the personal mantram. A person who has learned the art of mindfulness has also learned to die consciously. Here again we quote the great Shankaracharya:

> Now that I am about to die, may my *vayu* (wind) that is *prana*, leave this personality which is attached to Self, my great being to dwell with the Divine Self which is the Self of all, the immortal *Sutratman*, the thread joining all.
>
> May the subtle body, purified with knowledge and right actions, also ascend, for it alone has the capacity to seek guidance for the path. May this body be offered as an oblation into the fire and turn into ashes—OM.
>
> O you the source of volition, remember whatever I ought to remember as its time has arrived;
> O firey one, remember at this time all the actions I have performed since childhood.
>   —Isha Upanishad 17

When one can remember all one's physical, mental and vocal actions of the day, by way of introspection, before falling asleep at night, and when one can remember all such actions even which are performed during sleep, then at the hour of death one can gather the storehouse of memories and mold it in his own way, taking it along or leaving it behind.

Along with all these practices comes *japam*, the mental repetition of particular mantras especially the mantra of the Sun, also called the daughter of the Sun, or the guardian of the *pranas, gayatri*. Another mantra is known as the death-conquerer or *mrtyunjaya*. These mantras cannot be learned simply from books but must be received as part of the yoga initiatory processes, accompanied with appropriate experience of dying as imparted by the kind and compassionate Guru through his own willing grace. The translation of the *mrtyunjaya* mantra is as follows:

> I sacrifice unto the one who has three mothers, the
> three eyes, the fragrant one who increases nurture.
> Like a fruit from the vine may I be freed from death,
> not (separating) from immortality.

Hundreds of thousands of recitations, fire offerings of fragrant incense and herbs, may be made by way of prayer for a dying person. The yogi who has abandoned attachment to the body, practicing this mantra, will definitely attain freedom from death and return to the homeland of his immortal consciousness.

The true source of immortality, however, is only the kundalini, the ray of God dwelling within us. As laya yoga, the yoga of dissolution helps the spirit to dissolve the ties with mortal veils so the yoga of kundalini helps him to recognize immortality. This ray of God in the human being is not a metaphor, not a poetic term. Many times people read these words and say, "Ah, what a beautiful poetic thought" but these are used literally in the yoga science. This ray of light is located in the spine, flowing from the base of the spine up to the thousand-petal lotus, like a flash of pure white lightning, shining with the brilliance of ten thousand suns, but very narrow as though a ten thousandth part of a hair. Nachiketas, the seeker in the Katha Upanishad, was finally taught by Yama, the god of death:

as a person may carefully peel the fiber from a reed
in a straight line so the yogi gathers his prana and
carefully passes it through the Sushumna channel of
the kundalini; leading his entire consciousness upward, he then departs through the solar gate.
—Katha Upanishad 2, 3, 16, 17

The solar gate is the center of the sun with a thousand rays, the thousand-petal lotus, situated at the
fontanelle described above.

For this penetration through the solar gate, one
needs to have mastered the method of *bindhu-vedhana*,
piercing through the point. In this the entire consciousness
and life force is gathered together from each and all of
the systems within the personality into a single pinpoint
of light and awareness. Conscious migration by way of
death is a very simple step from there.

The science of voluntary migration from the time
body was brought to such perfection in the Himalayas that
the entire civilization of Tibet was centered around this
fact. The current Dalai Lama, the fourteenth incarnation
of the same soul is said to have taken the vow fourteen
incarnations ago to continue to be reborn to guide the
Tibetan nation. After each death various wise men of the
Council search out the new incarnation by looking for
certain signs. Similarly, the leaders of all great monasteries
continue to be reborn for guiding others. These wise men
assume their full monastic duties as philosophers, guides
and administrators by the age of twelve or thirteen because
they have already reached the highest wisdom in the previous life. Their education now is simply a process of
reawakening the reminiscences of this knowledge. Even
this author taught the Vedas to great swamis at the age of

thirteen and regards his present body simply a continuation of the karmic mission assumed in a previous life.

In the Buddhist tradition the aspiring personalities are divided into three categories:

Sotapanna, the stream-entered ones, those who have been already initiated and have picked up a momentum towards liberation.

Sakad-agami, those who will return to the body only once more.

Anagami, those who will return no more after their current body has died.

A *Bodhisattva*, however, is one who has taken the vow of returning again and again out of compassion until all the sentient beings have discarded their role of suffering and their robes of ignorance. Such great Buddhas choose their own place and time of rebirth after they have abandoned a dying body.

These liberated disincarnate masters may also guide other living beings without needing to resort to a physical body in some cases where those to be guided are properly attuned to their vibrations in one way or another. We read of Saul on the road to Damishk (Damascus) being touched with a lightning of *kundalini*, so that for three days and three nights he could not open his eyes to the external world and remained with the Consciousness of his Master. Similarly, H. H. Swami Rama has narrated the story in *Living with the Himalayan Masters* of when his own Master left the body yet spoke to his disciples.

The great Shankaracharya began his philosophical conquest of India at the age of sixteen when, following the traditions of Indian philosophers, he traveled to far corners in four directions of the compass and challenged the philosophers of various schools to debate. During his journeys he heard of the greatest philosopher of the Mimamsa school, by name Mandana Mishra. As he arrived on the outskirts of Mandana's village, he asked a lady fetching water from the village well the way to Mandana's house. She replied in beautiful Sanskrit verse:

> The universe is permanent, the universe is not permanent—
> where the parrots and the myna birds hung at the cages at the door
> discuss such matters among themselves, having heard them often—
> know that to be Mandana's house

> The scripture is self-evident, not self-evident—
> where the parrots and the myna birds hung at the cages at the door
> discuss such matters among themselves, having heard them often—
> know that to be Mandana's house.

Undaunted by the display of scholarship by a common woman, Shankaracharya found his way to the home of the great Brahmin philosopher who was at that time busy performing a ritual behind closed doors. Shankara, using his yoga power of *anima*, the siddhi of becoming minute, entered the chamber and surprised the philosopher. Finally a date was set for the debate. It was a rule that a neutral philosopher, familiar with both schools of philosophy, must become the judge to decide upon the winner at the end of the debate. It was Mandana's wife, the woman at the well, who was selected to be the neutral judge by agreement of both parties. Each day she sat in judgment without being partial to either side. Her own power of observation was such that one day when she had to be away from the debate on some errand, she asked both parties to continue the debate. Upon return from her errand, she said that her husband had been having difficulties with the debate. She had based this statement on the observation that her husband's garland was more withered which is the case with flowers when they are placed around the neck of an agitated as against a relatively calm person.

Finally, one day, she gave her judgment that Shankara had won and her husband had lost the debate.

No longer a judge, she was again a wife and said to Shankara: "You have won the debate only against the half of my husband; the other half, I, now challenge you to continue the debate." She manipulated the debate in such a manner that she involved Shankara in an argument concerning the secrets of *kamashastra*, the science of love, of which, he, a perfect celibate swami, knew nothing. At this point he requested a month's postponement of the continuation of the debate. Along with his disciples he came to a kingdom where the king was about to die. Shankara left his body in a cave guarded by his disciples and the physicians and counselors were surprised to note that the king who seemed dead suddenly revived and that there was a total change of character in him. He had become a saintly man. They did not know that it was Shankara's spirit which was now occupying the body of the dead king. In this body he learned all the secrets of the erotic science. The time was passing and one of the disciples came to the king's court and sang the hymn known as *mohamudgara*, a mace to beat the delusion with! This reminded Shankara to return to his body which he did. The debate was resumed and Shankara finally won.

The science of *para-kaya-pravesha*, entry into another body, is known only to a few yogis. Our own Gurudev, H. H. Swami Rama, makes mention of it in his *Living with the Himalayan Masters*. There are perhaps one or two such masters—whom we may have seen with our own eyes and not recognized—walking around in the body with which they were not born. An hour comes when the karma of that body has expired but the compassionate work of guiding other beings must continue. The yogi with the help of the Guru may take over the body of another dying person which may last longer. The science requires the total mastery of the karmic process and of the disciplines mentioned above. The master must also know the secret of recharging one-hundred and seven *marma-sthanas* of the body with *prana*. The word *marma* means the spot of death. There are thirty-eight points in the body, according to the ancient physicians, where *prana* becomes warped to cause disease. A hit at one of these *marmas* can be fatal. At the hour of death, the *prana* may become, as it were, stuck in one of these *marmas*, thus prolonging the agony. The yogi who enters the new body not only recharges all the other systems within the personality but also facilitates the free flow of *prana* through these thirty-eight *marmas*. Uncanny as it may seem, the process is not different from reincarnation but it saves much time so that an entirely new infantile body does not need to be trained and the volition of the yogi's spirit is in control from the moment of entry.

It is tragic that the Western mind equates immortality

with the survival and resurrection of the physical body. It is, however, the yogi who has such total control over his body processes that a person like the Gurudev Swami Rama of the Himalayas can demonstrate clinical death— and yet arise from that death. The yogi uses this self-discipline to prolong the lifespan until his mission here has been accomplished.

Only through strict discipline does one transform one's body as though in the crucible of an alchemist and gradually so masters its processes that death becomes a child's play. Not understanding that this alchemy was of the spirit and not only of the body, there arose in India also a philosophy known as the School of Rasa. The word *rasayana* is used in the texts of Ayurveda, the science of long life, the Indian medical science, both for chemistry as well as for the body alchemy. By the body alchemy are implied processes taught in some detail in these texts: the inner washes, special herbal baths, use of secret herbal extracts, dietary procedures under strict discipline over a period of time in such a way that the body of a one-hundred-year-old person is rejuvenated, teeth growing back, skin becoming smooth, facial appearance youthful and the gray or bald head turning black. It was felt by these alchemists of the body that the mastery of *rasa*, mercury, through certain alchemical and chemical procedures could restore the human body to its youthful state. These philosophers aspired to the immortality of the body while the great Tantric yogis of India who taught the art of celibacy understood the mercury and sulphur to be the *rasas* of the body itself, and not a mineral element.

The Vedas speak of one-hundred-one deaths such as

anger, grief, passion and frustration. In the *Aitareya Aranyaka* it is said that death took the form of *apana*, the lower *prana* and entered the sex organs. This, because the sex activity drains so much of our life force. The cumulative effect of all these little deaths is what we ordinarily view as the final death.

The unbridled license given to emotions is a major cause of our diseases. The individual mind constantly in a state of emotional disturbance dissipates most of its energy. Only a calm mind can draw the universal *prana*, the vital force, into the personality. The entire Prashna Upanishad is dedicated to answering six questions on *prana*. We paraphrase Shankaracharya's commentary on this Upanishad (12.3):

> Prana, drawn from the supreme self, comes to operate in this body through the actions of the mind. Prana is the Lord, like an emperor over its fivefold divisions operating in the active senses. It has external connections such as with the sun, and the internal ones such as with the cognitive senses. He who understands this prana attains immortality.

Through the dissipation of mental energy, the *prana* energy is lost. The perceptions become dull. Unseen warps, energy deficiencies, pockets of negative charge, appear in various parts of the brain, the nervous system, various internal organs, the *marmas*, and the very cells. Such weakening of energy over a period of time has the cumulative effect of producing disease—leading to death. We become aware of the cessation of breath at death but forget that the continuous process of the weakening of *prana* through disturbed emotional states causes irregularity of breath. These irregularities show their cumulative effect in the final cessation of breath.

The yogis practice celibacy not as a denial of pleasure but as a quieting of agitation. They have made discoveries regarding the state of breath which may appear startling to an average individual. For example, it is known to every student of yoga that one nostril exhales actively while the other remains passive, and that the nostrils change their roles in every one hour and forty minutes to two hours. One of the few rare and brief moments when both nostrils flow actively is during sexual climax. Because a spark of the parents' *prana* and the mind force is to be transferred to a new being about to be conceived, such total balance of the prana and the mind-force is essential.

Now, the yoga tradition does not believe that the human lifespan is karmically measured in terms of a number of years but rather in the number of breaths. By maintaining agitated states of mind, we shorten our breaths; we spend them out in less time which can be easily extended by deepening the breath through nurturing quieter states of mind. The pleasure derived in sexual climax is not in agitation but concentration of mind and the *prana*-force, that results in both nostrils flowing equally. The yogi, however, enjoys an internal ecstasy of *samadhi* for hours and days at a time. When he is in *samadhi* both his nostrils flow evenly for hours and days at a time—without any agitation. So the yogis state that the pleasure of sex is not even a fraction of the ecstasy of meditation during which the upward implosions in the *sushumna* channel of *kundalini* bring us a soothing touch of the universal Mother. Celibacy becomes easier and more enjoyable than sex.

Repeated sex acts reduce our lifespan and bring

death closer in the following manner. Take a breath cycle
to be of two hours. If a sexual climax occurs, say, at one
hour during the left nostril cycle, and both nostrils are
activated during the climax, the rest of the left nostril
cycle is never completed. Immediately after the climax the
right nostril takes over. (That is why people turn over on
the other side.) The rest of the hour is lost, never regained;
the lifespan is reduced by one hour. That hour's worth
of energy is dissipated.

Constant sexual thought as well as fantasy also
disturbs the breath, dissipates the mind-energy and above
all makes the mind flesh-bound. Freedom from this flesh
at the hour of death becomes difficult to attain. Thus it
is said:

> Through the ascetic discipline of celibacy
> the wise gods conquered death.
> —Arharva-Veda XI. 5. 19

The wise gods, *devas*, are the shining ones, the
masters who have access to the jar of *amrta*, the nectar
of immortality. This nectar of immortality is said to have
been obtained by them by churning the cosmic ocean for
many aeons.

The alchemists who sought to duplicate this nectar
for attaining immortality of the body forgot that juices,
rasas, of the body were not mercury and sulphur but the
sexual fluid, *virya* in man and *rajas* in woman, which only
a celibate completely masters and conquers. Through a
spiritual alchemy such a celibate uses the sexual force so
as to make it ascend through the *sushumna* stream of
kundalini until it rises to the thousand-petal lotus, there
to become *ojas*, the quintessence of all the *rasas* of life.

Ojas then imparts freedom from sickness and the aging process; not immortality of the body but the power over death so the yogi enters volitional death only after he has lived as long as he wishes to accomplish his particular mission in life.

It has been customary for all great masters before dying to take a bath and change their clothing, sit down and chat with their disciples. Great yogis have announced their hour of death years and years before. They look hale and hearty but the word goes out to all the important disciples. "Come, the Master wants to say farewell." Everyone gathers and the master sits down in his lotus posture, gives his last sermon, feeds the beloved disciples with his own hands like an Indian or a Jewish mother feeding an offspring and then says goodbye. He sits there, draws his breath and passes out. Paramahansa Yogananda, author of *Autobiography of a Yogi* gave a big feast. After the banquet he said, "Well friends, it's time for me to go. Goodbye." Thus he gets up and dies on them!

A swami that is an ordained monk is not cremated. When a person takes the vow of swamihood, he performs unto himself, to his past personality, the rites that are normally performed by relatives following a kin's death and cremation. The swami dies unto himself, then takes a baptismal dip in the waters of a sacred river, to be reborn as he emerges. So, upon his physical death the idiom used is not of dying, but that he has taken *samadhi*. Their graves are also thus referred to as the *samadhi* of such and such swami or the saint.

There is more to such a phrase than a mere idiom. The swamis, and even householder yogis, but only those

who are masters of the art of dying, often declare before-
hand the time of their departure from the world.
Sometimes they take *jala-samadhi*—go into the water not
to emerge again as was done by Swami Rama Tirtha.

What sort of qualification in life is needed to accomplish that for death is illustrated by a story of Swami
Dayanand Saraswati. When he was attacked by two rogues
on a river bank, he grabbed them each by an arm, jumped
into the river and sat down at the bottom! The yogi may,
however, choose to take *sthala-samadhi*, to have his body
absorbed in the earth. At the appointed hour he orders a
grave dug, sits down at the bottom in meditation with
instruction to have the grave filled up with salt and then
clay. Since there are now scientifically proved instances of
yogis surviving in airtight boxes, it is not difficult to
assume that the yogi may remain in *samadhi* in the grave
for some time and then relinquish the body at will. The
sites of such *samadhis* are extremely sacred.

About 150 miles from Bombay, near the city of
Pune, is a temple commemorating a spot where a child-
saint named Jnana-deva had taught. He began his adult
life at thirteen when he set his meditation and teaching
seat at this particular spot. Thousands of people flocked
daily to hear him recite his extempore verse translation
and spiritual commentary on the Bhagavad-gita in the
spoken language of the people. Up to his time the text was
open only to Sanskrit scholars. At the age of eighteen he
is said to have completed his work. His message was all
given. He ordered a *samadhi* (grave?) dug, had it filled with
salt, sat in it in the state of *samadhi*. The earth is poured
over him—and yet today thousands of people visit the

temple where Jnana-deva had taught seven centuries ago.

This author was brought up on the stories of the holy sites where some of his own ancestors entered such *samadhi*. One grave, the *khwaja sharif* of a Sufi Muslim saint in the city of Ajmer is visited by thousands of people; merely touching the grave is said to impart to one a feeling of sublime tranquility and peace. Such yogis teach thus even in death. The Buddha said to his disciples: "If anyone has a question let him ask now; do not let them say that the Buddha departed leaving some doubts without clearing them!"

There are many other ways in which the yogis are said to have renounced their bodies. One is *agni-samadhi*: through intense concentration a flame is manifested from the fire-chakra in the navel center and the entire body is thus consumed. Many women of absolutely chaste character are said to have resorted to this method when they were prevented from climbing into the fire of a husband's funeral pyre. These women are still honored by the title of *sati*, feminine form of the Sanskrit word for a saint. The whole of India is dotted by the sacred spots honoring these *satis*.

One of the most enviable ways to depart is to merge into the Deity one worships. The great seventeenth century lady, Saint Mira, is an example. She drank a poison cup that was given her falsely stating that it was *prasada*, remnants of a worship offering to the Lord. "What has been once termed an offering to the Lord cannot be poison for Mira" she said and drank it. Many years later she is said to have merged into the light that appeared from the image of Krishna in her private temple. Another lady saint, Andal Ranganayaki, wedded the Lord Ranganatha (God worshipped as the Lord of all that is colorful, and entertaining and sweet in the theatre of the universe), climbed up to the reclining image and two lights were seen merging together. Chaitanya Mahaprabhu, the greatest saint of Bengal in the sixteenth century, similarly merged with the image of Lord Jagannatha (Master of the Universe). Manikavachakar merged into the image of Nataraja (Lord of the dance of the Universe) at the famous temple called Chid-ambaram (Lord wearing consciousness as clothing).

The miraculous stories of such merger with the divine manifestations may seem beyond modern man's credibility. But this statement underestimates the modern man's capacity for faith. Are there not millions of people today who believe that the spirit of Christ is present at the Eucharist. There can, then, be no problem in accepting that divine light makes itself manifest wherever the devotees seek it, and adore it in all sincerity.

There are three greatest possible aspirations of a spiritual person:

> may no one be born in my generation who does not know God;
>
> may I attain enlightenment in this life;
>
> even if I do not attain full enlightenment this life, may I die in meditation.

Recall here again the words of Solon the Greek lawgiver referred to earlier. The last moments of a saint reflect his entire life. St. Francis of Assisi awaited the arrival of "sister death," and asked the brothers to "throw ashes on my brother body"—which they did; and then he sang with them . . . "Take my soul out of prison . . . " and then lay back.

When his mission is complete, often a great Master announces the date of his departure much in advance. A word goes out to the disciples to gather. Like a mother, the Guru feeds his disciples, gives much joy through his laughter, much wisdom with the answers to a few questions. Then he bids farewell and goes into *samadhi* from which he will not arise. As H. H. Swami Rama states, it is an honor to be present at the occasion of such a Master's Great Departure. For more advanced details, read Swamiji's *Living with the Himalayan Masters.*

The Yoga of Dissolution

We have said before that laya-yoga teaches the art of dissolving the material attachments and the kundalini-yoga grants the realization of the immortality of the spirit. Much has been written about kundalini-yoga but little experienced by most except by only a few blessed ones who have died at the hand of their Master, and are reborn in spirit. The branch known as laya-yoga is seldom mentioned independently. Here I would like to describe this system briefly.

A great sage asked his young son to leave the forest ashram to travel and learn the secrets of yoga from King Janaka of the city of Mithila. This is the same king in whose court Yajnavalkya so often demonstrated his philosophical supremacy. When the young boy arrived from the forest ashram at the king's palace, he was surprised and shocked. He thought: Why did my father send me here to this king who lives in a luxurious palace surrounded by young maidservants? Certainly, this king must know nothing of the life of asceticism without which the secrets of metaphysics cannot be learned. If he is such a wise man why does he live in such palaces in the company of beautiful maidens? While the young boy was thus arguing in his mind, he was invited to the king's presence.

"Would you like to take a guided tour around this palace?" the king offered.

"Yes, certainly, your majesty," the young man was more than eager. The king ordered the young man to hold in his hand a bowl filled with oil to the brim. Two guards with naked swords were commanded to walk behind him while the young boy was being escorted through the palace. He was told to be careful in carrying the bowl of oil. Not a single drop must spill or he would lose his head. The tour was thus completed and the party returned to the king's palace.

"Did you enjoy the tour? Did you like my palace?" the king asked.

"Enjoy the tour, indeed! How could I enjoy the tour with death hanging over my shoulder in the form of naked swords in the hands of your guards. I was busy watching the drop of oil so I could not even lift my eyes up to see your palace," retorted the young man.

"Quite correctly so," said the king. "When you are aware of death watching over your shoulder you have scarce little moment to look at palaces and beautiful maidens. A doubt had arisen in your mind as to the wisdom of your father in sending you here, to a king who lives in a luxurious palace surrounded by beautiful maidens; but I live only to perform my actions. My duties of watching over my subjects require me to live here but I live as though without a body, a body which may be snatched by death at any moment. Not a single drop of the oil of time must I spill, and this alone is the reason that your father has sent you here."[1]

The first step is the dissolution of the gross elements into the finer elements; the grosser aspects of the physical personality merging into the finer aspects of the physical personality, and then leading on to the entry into the subtle body.

The second step in laya-yoga is the dissolution of breath rhythms from grosser rhythms into the finer rhythms. In the science of *svara*, the science of breath rhythms, there are levels known as of earth, water, fire, air and space. There is an earth breath, water breath, the fire breath, and so on, depending on how well the person has refined his *prana* and awakened his breathing process. Each one of these levels has certain geometrical figures associated with it in the mind from which the entire science of *Mandala* or yoga of psychocosmic geometrical designs have developed, including the various colors of the elements.

The third step is the dissolution of the various elements and aspects *within* the subtle body.

The fourth step is identical to kundalini-yoga, the elevation of the *kundalini* force from the lower centers gradually to the higher centers. As this elevation occurs the experience changes. When one finally dissolves and raises and merges the lower centers of consciousness into the higher centers, there comes for him a cosmic vision of Mahakala, the vision of the great time, the mega-time or the meta-time, of Mahakali, the beauty of the three worlds.

These visions are described briefly in the ninth through eleventh chapters of the Bhagavad-gita; in the greatest metaphysical text of 27,000 verses known as the Yoga-Vasishtha; and in the major text of the Superconscious Meditation tradition, the Saundarya-Lahari. It is the vision of cosmic dissolution.

When the vision of cosmic dissolution occurs, the yogi is now in touch with the process of creation and dissolution of the entire universe, in which the individual body is the tiniest of the possible specks. In the cycle of creation and dissolution going on for billions upon billions of years, the time vision expands. As it expands the attachment to the limited time of a single lifespan vanishes. The consciousness now sees everything in terms of a cosmic scale like the one described earlier as a single glance of the Mother Divine. Immediately the yogi is elevated from the level of humanity to the level of divinity. The body-bound person views the world in this order: the physical body within the concrete creation, which is within space, which is continuing within time. A *videha* sees the creation of time, then of space, then the concrete universe within which he finds the proper proportions of his own physical being. He is bodiless because he now guides the seeking souls through mind-power or by spoken word according to whatever vibration level they are attuned to. Only for this reason he maintains a physical body.

Another aspect of laya-yoga is concerned with the practices of nada-yoga, the yoga of sound, so that the yogi merges grosser sound vibrations into subtle sound vibrations.

Finally we come to the process of *prakriti-laya*; the entire material of the universe is derived from *prakrti* which is a state of equilibrium of *sattva, rajas* and *tamas*. These three categories can be studied in detail by reading the Bhagavad-gita, chapters 14, 17 and 18. This is the basis of the Sankhya system of philosophy. When *sattvas, rajas* and *tamas* are disturbed, a dis-equilibrium occurs, which is the beginning of creation. And *prakrti*, the dynamic field of equilibrium, sends forth material for the mass of the universe (*mahat*) as well as for cosmic ego (*ahamkara*). Personal ego, the mind, the senses, the subtle and physical body, and the five sheaths are derived from the same disturbed mass and ego. The yogi, through progressive stages in developing equanimity, finally reaches the state of total mental equilibrium. For him the entire universe is then dissolved though it continues to exist as normal for those whose vision has not yet changed. The yogi no longer views the disequilibrium as such but only sees *prakrti*, the equilibrium of all. His chief mode of operation then becomes the causal body, *karana-sharira*. Thereafter he functions only in cosmic time and sees all things of the past and the future as present, nothing hindering his vision. His horizons now being so vast that "He now marches to some other drum." Such a being is thereafter known as a *jivan-mukta*, living, liberated. His body looks like that of any ordinary human but it is now only a channel for unlimited consciousness. He has reached apotheosis. From that moment on, death does not exist.

Be born a human being; die a god. Till you reach a godhood at least aim at:

dying for an unselfish cause, or
dying in meditation
but not dying bound and pitifully crying. One has to work
for one's freedom. When this freedom comes, when from
the other shore the Being of Light calls you, you have
already reached the state of apotheosis and your light
merges with Light.

On the following pages, I lead you through a beginner's exercise in laya-yoga.

After the first nine exercises in *shava-asana* relaxa-
tions
Breathe out all impurities.
Breathe out all your tensions, worries and problems.
Resolve in your mind that
I surrender the fruits of this meditation to the
Supreme Consciousness Force, to the Supreme
Life Force.
I surrender this very meditation to the guru spirit
that flows through me whenever I empty my mind
to receive the grace of the purity of meditation.
Let this thought, let this feeling, let this emotion flow
through you at this moment.
Surrender the awareness of your body to a higher aware-
ness.
Relax your body and let go of it.
Bring your awareness to your breathing.
Focus your entire mind on the feel of the breath.
Feel each movement of the breath.
Feel the progress of the flow of the breath moment by
moment.

Feel every micromoment of your breath in the nostril.
Let there be no break in your breathing as though your
mantram is a silent echo, a resonance through the entire
space of your body.
Know that your breath is the contact between the divine
infinity and your own being.
Breathe as though your breath flows out and in,
        not only within the body.
Inhale from your toes as though the breath is going all the
way from your body out into infinity, and your exhala-
tions going from the crown all the way into infinity.
Interwoven with your mantram,
        your breath,
        now knows,
        no end . . .
        flows from every pore of the body,
        merges with infinity,
        from the crown of your head,
        from your toes,
        flowing out and flowing in,
        without a pause.
Wherever you go your mantram goes with you.
Exhale and inhale as though infinity breathes through you.
Inhale and exhale as though your breath flows out from
your toes
        from the crown of your head,
        expanding into the infinite,
        unlimited space,
        with your mantram.
Observe all that is of the earth within you;
all that is of the solids in your personality;

all that is solid in the flesh,
    in the bones,
    in the particles
    in the cells of your body.
From your skull to your toes, in the front, in the back, on
your sides;
Observe the surfaces of your skin, of the entire body:
    front, back and sides,
    hidden parts between fingers and toes,
    thighs, armpits,
    from the skull to the soles of your feet.
Open your skin mentally and observe what is inside the
skin, the raw red being. Make yourself skinless. What is
inside the skin from the skull to your soles of the feet,
observe that:
    all the blood vessels, capillaries,
    all the cells of your body.
Observe what is underneath the skin in your skull, on your
forehead:
    Remove the skin of your eyelids, of the eyes and
    see what you have.
    Remove the skin of your rosy cheeks,
    of the nostrils,
    of your mouth.
Observe your neck from your shoulders down to your
finger tips:
    your front, your chest, and the breast, and the
    nipples.
Remove the skin and observe the insides.
Observe your lungs.
Observe the esophagus.

Observe the trachea.
Observe your heart muscle.
Observe the red blood flowing through your entire being.
Observe the contents of your stomach in the state that they are now.
Observe the various stages of the contents of your internal organs.
Observe all the phlegm within you.
Observe all that you eliminate that is within you.
Again remove the surfaces of your skin:
> from your stomach, navel, and abdomen,
> remove the surfaces of the skin,
> and see the underneath;
> from your thighs, knees,
> remove the skin;
> from your calves, ankles, feet and toes,
> remove the skin.

Here you lie bare, skinless.
Observe the entire being from top to toe as it is hidden inside the skin.
Let this pulsating mass,
> throbbing,
> continue to breathe.

Exhale and inhale with your mantram as though your breath is going all the way into infinity.
Observe it flowing through your entire mass of blood vessels and bonds,
> your prana,
> throbbing,
> vibrating.

Observe it flowing through all your internal organs as you

have viewed them in their openness and nakedness, without the covering of the skin, all the way, every limb, from the skull to the toes.

Let all your blood vessels peel off.

Let the network of arteries, veins and capillaries dry up; all fall off.

Let the network of all your nerves shrivel away and vanish.

Yet there remains the awareness of you that breathes with the mantram.

Let all the muscles vanish as though you are bare bones.

Let all the internal organs, from the organs of elimination and generation to your cardiac center and the heart, disappear.

Let your lungs vanish.

Let the flesh around your neck and face disappear.

Here lies a skeleton enwrapping an empty space.

Exhale and inhale as though the breath is flowing through the empty spaces in the skeleton, and the consciousness is filled only with the mantram.

Previously, where your consciousness was filled with your organs, nerves, capillaries, veins and other structures,

>now the consciousness and the life force is freed,
>and your life force and your consciousness force
>goes out with this breath,
>and the mantram flowing not only through
>the spaces in the skeleton, but all the
>way into eternity,
>all the way into infinity,
>on all sides.

From this skeleton remove your feet, fling them away into an empty space.

Continue to exhale and inhale into infinity with your mantram.

Remove your bones from the knees down to your ankles from this skeleton, and throw them away into endless space to vanish.

Take your thigh bones, cast them away.
Fling them into empty space far away
from where they will not return.
Take off the pelvic bones.
Throw them away; only the end of the
spine remains.

Continue to inhale and exhale into infinity.
Cast away with an effort of your will,
your rib cage.
Throw it away.

From the skeleton, with an effort of your will, let the arms move,
vanish somewhere into endless space.

See what an empty skull looks like.
You have that skull and your spinal bone.
Separate the skull and exhale it away.

Your consciousness, your life force, your mantra, your prana, your subtle body—yet remain.

Exhale and inhale; for, you and your ray of consciousness the sushumna is here, one with the sushumna and the kundalini of the whole universe.

Exhale and inhale.
You the bodiless being,
this pure Self you are,
stretching out from infinity to infinity.
Your prana flows,

the awareness of your mantra flows,
from infinity to infinity,
curving back to you through infinity.
Let there be no break as the prana force flows through
your subtle body.

When the force of your samskaras is too strong it binds
you. It brings back for you another physical body. You
want to remain bound to limited consciousness, alas;
    alas, you return to this body and
    cherish it as though it were eternal, pure, Self, and
    as though its beauty were its own.
Exhale and inhale again.
Breathe as though your body is whole and you are a
reincarnated being.
Exhale and inhale through all the points of the blue star
with your mantram from the skull to the soles,
flowing out into infinity.
Again you begin your journey to liberate your own being
from the false bondage of
    limited time,
    limited space,
    limited causation,
    to which your physical body is bound,
    the body to which you have bound your
    unlimited life force, your
    unlimited consciousness force.
Exhale and inhale with your mantram from the skull to
the soles and beyond into infinity.

Observe the existence of this earth.

Observe all earth in the universe, all things that are solid, and all the planets, including this earth.

Observe all that is of the earth in you; all that is of the solids in your physical body.

From head to toe realize that all these solids are the same as the rest of the earth.

> These solids have come to me from the earth.
>
> I am not these solids.
>
> They are not mine.
>
> I merge them back into the earth, their origin.

Know that the solids of your cells, of your vessels, of your organs, of your bones and flesh are one with the ashes of the earth.

Exhale and inhale as though your breath is flowing through this heap of ashes shaped as the human body.

When the consciousness remains with the mantram,

the life force simply observes this man,

this woman made of ashes.

Let the force of your prana scatter these ashes.

> Let the breezes and winds of your breath
>
> scatter them away.
>
> Let the ashes go and mingle with the ashes
>
> of all of the earth element in the whole
>
> universe.

You do not cease to be. Your ashes expand and become one and your consciousness now dwells in all earth and in all the earths that have ever been, that shall ever be from infinity to infinity. For, you have freed yourself from the time zone to the infinite.

Continue as a being of light, life and consciousness.

Exhale and inhale with your mantram.

Your breath passes into the infinity in all directions.
The force of your samskaras contracts you from infinity
to this finite being again,
> alas . . .

Observe the flux of the universe.
Bring your mind to the flux of the galaxies.
See all that is of the waters within you;
> See all that is of the wetness within you,
> from the skull to the soles,
> all the fluids in which you have floated,
> inside the mother's womb.
Those waters permeate you.
Observe the fluids in which your brain floats,
> the fluidity of the brain itself.
Observe the water in your tear ducts.
Observe the waters in your bloodstream
> flowing, coursing through many hundred
> kilometers of a network of veins,
> and arteries,
> and capillaries,
> and blood vessels.
From head to toe observe the waters of the blood
being channeled by the heart.
> Observe the waters of your saliva.
> Observe the wetness in your trachea,
> in your esophagus,
> in your lungs.
Observe the wetness of your food being digested in the
stomach and throughout the internal organs.
Observe the putrid collection of waters in the bladder.

Exhale and inhale as though the breath is flowing through
all the waters of your body,
with your mantram, going out into infinity.
Observe the flux of infinity.
Observe the flux of time, the flux of the universe, the
flux of all the galaxies,
      the flowing waters of the sacred milky way.
Observe the waters in all the clouds around this planet.
Observe all the waters in all the oceans, their entire extent,
entire depth.
Observe all the waters in all the waterfalls, in the sub-
terranean rivers, in all the streams flowing within the
womb of the earth and of the mountains. Let your breath
follow them.
Let the waters of your body be one with all the waters in
every mighty river,
      every pool on this earth, including the pool
      of your bladder, the pool in which the fluid
      of your brain floats, the pools of waters in
      your blood vessels;
Let your breath flow through all the waters, without
differentiating among the waters of the body, waters of
the planet, waters of the universe; the flux of the whole
universe, flowing in time, and beyond time into infinity.

Let all your personal waters emerge through the universal
waters into the flux of infinity, and
      exhale and inhale, with your mantram.
Let all your waters evaporate and become one with the
universe.
Let your attachments to all tastes vanish.

Say

> these fluids are not mine.
> Merge them into their origins.
> I am not these waters.

Exhale and inhale, Your samskaras are becoming finer, they are seeking finer aspects of your personal being.

Your person is no longer of the earth. All your attachments for fragrances have vanished. All your aversions for any other smells have vanished. All your attractions and aversions to taste have vanished. You are now free of those temptations.
Observe the fires of the galaxies and stars.
Observe the fire that burns in the sun,
Take a dip in this solar fire.
Be aware of the fire that is in lightning and in thunder.
Become aware of the forest fires,
Fires burning in the hearths.
Become aware of the fires which are the flames on altars.
Become aware of the fire as all-pervading;
Heat and light all around you is also fire,
Know the fire in your personality;
You come, come to a personality made of fires as though your entire body is a flame. Your breath and the mantram are flowing through this flame. Flowing through this flame from the skull to the soles. All the way into infinity.
Observe the heat and the warmth of this flame that is imparted to the earth and the waters of this body.
Observe the fires in the generative organs, flaming no longer outwards but inward, into the path of the kundalini.

Observe the fires of digestion, the red flame that burns in your navel, invisible, and digests the food that is eaten and converts that which was not of the person into an integral part of the person.

Observe the fires here, making engines of the internal organs moving, working. Observe the fires in your heart center.

Observe the fires of speech, that flame out from your thought and from your vocal cords.

Observe the fires in your eyes.

Observe your brain cells firing, a kaleidoscope of the colors of your thought and sparks of the fire passing the synapses in hundreds and thousands of nerves through your entire being. Observe the fires, electric sparks and the lightnings in your brain cells. All of the sparks are a part of this flame that is your person.

Exhale and inhale as though your breath, flowing through all these fires is going out into the fire of infinity.

Fires flaming in the gems that are under the ground.

Fires in the molten core of this earth.

Fires burning forests

Observe the fires kindled by priests for sacrifice. Flaming upwards.

Take one of these fires, mingle your flame of the person with one of these fires, flaming upwards. The flame merging with the light and the sky, reaching out, becoming one with the lightning and thunder. Beyond, reaching out, through eons upon eons of space, becoming one with the fires in the heart of the sun, which is so puny, a purifier, compared with the fires of all the galaxies upon galaxies.

Numerous as hairs in the body of God. Let your fires
mingle, become one with these universal fires: your
breath and your mantram reaches out as a fiery being and
now you are part of this universal fire.

Breathe as though your breath is flowing through all of
these fires with your mantram.

And then the consuming fires at the end of a universe
when the galaxies fall into galaxies, where suns are shattered into suns, where planets are conflagrations, where
then will be the tiny sparks of the fire of your brain
cells? Let that be here and now. This merger.

Exhale and inhale as though all the cosmic fires are breathing through you and come alive with the life force that is
you.

The fires of the entire cosmos, recite your mantram.

Burn, burn, burn; flaming fire, burn.

Now I, the life force, untouched by you, observe this
game of the flames in the whole universe and in this little
person.

    The fire is not mine.

    I am not this fire. I merge it into its origins.

In these fires countless of your samskaras are being burned,
but not fully. Your other samskaras bring you down into
this tiny person, in its puny time scale, and you find your
consciousness dragged down again. But observe, you are no
longer a being of earth alone, of this person; nor of waters
alone of this person, nor of the fires alone of this person.

Observe the mighty wind of atoms flowing in the whole
cosmos.

Winds encircling this entire earth; observe.
Observe the air flowing in this empty space.
Observe the breezes moving leaves, leave out not a single
tree, leave out not a single leaf, leave out not a single
blade of grass, around this earth.
Observe the air in all the jars, in all the vessels and chalices.
Observe the winds and the breezes entering caves.
Observe that very air, entering through the cavities of
your body, the tiny caves.

> Here the air enters every cavity, every pore, and
> pours into you the force of prana as you exhale
> and inhale. Your breath is one with all the mighty
> airs. It is the same breath going into the cavity of
> your nostril, through your breathing channels into
> your sponge-like lungs, into your stomach all the
> way under your navel; going out, going in, into
> every tiny part of your being; entering the open-
> ings of every cell of your body—all the way from the
> skull to the soles.

So, exhale and inhale as though this breath is no longer of
the person but is just a whiff of the cosmic breeze, the
life-force and the consciousness-force that grabs and binds
to itself this whiff, remains and gives a direction of will.
The mantram flows as the silent sound of this breeze
which is one with the whole universe. You are a whiff of
breeze, know this whiff to the part of all winds and only
exhale and inhale with your mantram.

> This air is not mine.
> I am not this air. I am not this breath. I merge it
> into its origins.

The force of your samskaras will not remain one with all

the winds of the universe. It brings you back down to this false personality which you consider to be "I" without the possibility of this disintegration. But you are rising, the pilgrim within you is moving on to finer elements.

Observe all the spaces in the universe, vast spaces.
Feel the empty space around you;
> this empty space that is in the universe,
> this empty space that is around you continues into you.

Observe the empty spaces in your personality.
Observe all the empty spaces in this person, empty space of each pore, empty spaces between cells and cells; observe the spaces between your toes, spaces between your hairs, empty spaces in the palms, empty spaces between your fingers.
Observe the empty spaces in your armpits, observe the empty spaces inside your ears.
Observe the emptiness inside your skull, observe the emptiness in the cavities of your eyes, observe the emptiness in the cavities of your nostrils and sinuses, above the palate.
> Travel these paths.

Observe the emptiness of the palate, emptiness of the mouth, emptiness, yes, that your life-force, your consciousness-force occupies.
Observe the emptiness of your trachea, your esophagus, feel the emptiness in the holes in the sponge of your lungs; travel through those empty spaces.
Observe the emptiness in your stomach, the emptiness where your digestive tracts are not filled with putrid stuff.
Observe the emptiness inside your navel, emptiness in all

your internal organs. Observe the empty areas in your organs of elimination and generation. They are empty spaces of no consequence, empty spaces between all your cells. Observe all the empty spaces through kilometers upon kilometers of veins and arteries, through which emptiness, your blood courses. Observe the emptiness in the hollows of your bones. See the emptiness around this body; see the emptiness in all the spaces between planets and planets.

Empty spaces are curving out around the gravity pull of all the massive bodies of suns and galaxies, reaching out, reaching out. Go on a journey, on the exploration of this outer space, how far can you go. Remove from the spaces now, all the planets, all the suns, all the galaxies; so you have traveled beyond these now. You are aware of space which is far, far away where the light of the mightiest galaxy traveling at an incredible speed no longer reaches. In this space you are one, alone, only a being of life, a being of consciousness. Know all else to be empty.

Concentrate your mind on the emptiness of space.
The space inside your skull . . . is empty.
        Fill it with the force known as Intelligence, and
        awareness.
        Fill the space with awareness, with the light of
        Intelligence.
This empty space is continuing from the skull into the nostril.

Focus this Intelligence that is in the empty space,
    focus it onto a mantra,
    your mantra,
    vibrating in the Intelligence,
    flowing through the emptiness of the void of space,
    from the skull outwards, through the empty hollows
    of the nostrils,
    and flowing back again.
Be aware only of this emptiness, this space and this
Intelligence focused as the mantra; the rest has
relaxed and surrendered.
If any other thoughts arise send them out and away from
this emptiness.
    Send them away by relaxing your body.
The emptiness inside your skull is filled with Intelligence
focused on the mantra, flowing through the space known
as the nostrils.

This is you, the being of Intelligence, just the pure
Intelligence.
Your attachments to fragrances, aversions to smells have
vanished.
Your attachments to the taste of waters have gone, so have
aversions to all tastes.
Your attractions and aversions to forms seen in the light of
fire have been burned off. Your attraction and aversions to
all touches of winds and breezes on the skin are no more.
All sounds vanish.

The universe is dissolved; there is no more space, there is
no more time. You, the consciousness-force, you jiva, are

one with Brahman, infinite light, absolute, still, untouched. Time has been consumed, spaces have been voided; they have mingled with their origin in Consciousness. It is not a cosmic consciousness, for, the cosmos is no more; an absolutely pure being remains, and utterly joyful silence. Here there is no existence nor nonexistence. No motion, for there is no space

no time,

no timelessness.

Without word you the Brahman, know: I am Brahman, free, liberated, a being of will, knowledge, potency.

A being of totality of existence,

Consciousness, bliss and perfection.

Know: I am that, I am that, I am that.

Alas, you have samskaras that bring you back to this puny time,

this moment,

this place,

this skeleton,

these cavities,

this breath,

this warmth,

these fires,

these liquids,

these waters,

these blood vessels,

this skin,

these bones.

Then, inhale and exhale. Bound in this cage, the bird of your prana flutters, flies up and down and cries out for its freedom through the mantram.

Before the creation, and after the dissolution this life-force, this consciousness-force alone remains even when the spaces are dissolved into where space and time have no existence. But alas, the force of your samskaras make this far corner of the outer space curve back and you find yourself here, in your personal spaces, in your personal cavities to which you are so drawn. The cavities of your nostrils, of your mouth, of your skull, of your stomach, of your generative organs, these cavities draw you so that you lose sight that these puny spaces are just tiny imagined fractions of the vast spaces that you have just traversed.

Well, then, come back to the skeleton.
Recall the skeleton that you are with the skin peeled off. What are you, with your blood vessels dried up? Throw it away? thrown off, a being of ashes cast to ashes, this skeleton—what is it? Is this you, the Self?
Continue exhaling and inhaling with your mantram as though your breath is flowing through the empty spaces of this skeleton, the space that this skeleton encompasses.
Then take your feet, feet of this skeleton bones, throw them away.
Take off the bones from your knees to your ankles, fling them away into empty spaces. Let your subtle body continue to observe the flow of prana and of the mantram.
Take the thigh bones from your skeleton;
throw them away.
Take the bones of your pelvis from the skeleton; let your prana continue to observe the mantram, throw away the bones of the pelvis. All that remains is the end of your

spine there. Let the breath, prana and mantram continue to flow.

Take your rib cage, pluck it; throw it away into the space. Your subtle body continues to breathe with the mantram. Let your subtle body send forth a flash of will and cast off the bones of your hand and arms from this skeleton; you see it flung away into vast and mighty spaces to be lost. The life-force continues, the subtle body observes the flow of prana in the mantram. Let the will of the subtle body remove the skull, throw it away like a ball. It strikes the wall of infinity in space and is shattered.

Exhale and inhale, as though your whole body breathes with your mantram. Return to the samskara, this cycle of birth, death, pain, pleasure, action, consequence, but

from this moment on, use this body only
for action and not for the fruits of
action. Only then the force of your
samskaras will so diminish that when
Infinity calls you, your samskaras will
not drag you down again.

Watch your breath, enjoy this silence.

Gently, bring your fingertips to your eyelids and open your eyes to your palms. Join your hands and bow your head, with all the love of the heart, all the power of action in the hand, all the thoughts in the head. Worship the Deity who is within you.

NOTES
CHAPTER 7

1. This king, Janaka, is also known as *Videha*, the bodiless one. A master, though incarnate, may live as though disincarnate, not bound to the body at all. The Yoga-sutras speak of the masters known as *Videhas* and this word is the introduction to the philosophy of laya-yoga, the yoga of dissolution of matter.

Conclusion

The monks of the swami orders are by rule possessionless. Whatever they own is for the benefit of others, or they own nothing. The whole world is their family and wherever they are at the sunset is their home. They stay longer than a night at one place only if their mission requires it. Wherever they go their needs are taken care of by the community.

Once upon a time a wandering swami made his dwelling in a ruin outside a village. The villagers flocked to listen to him. One family took it upon themselves to provide his evening meals. The parents would send the meal every evening by their young son. Daily the boy would arrive at the ruin out of breath, looking shaky, pale and scared. After a few days the fatherly swami inquired as to the reason for this. The boy said, "Sire, no one has told you this but on the way from the village to this ruin there is a haunted tree. The ghost there chases me every time I come this way; I am scared and have to run for my life."

Now, some of the swamis keep a sacred fire in which they burn many fragrant herbs; it keeps mosquitoes and animals away. The ashes are rubbed on the body for protection and may be used for healing. The Swami said, "I have done much chanting and praying over this fire. Its ashes are very potent. Here, take this handful and keep it with you. When you come this way tomorrow and the ghost chases after you, make sure that you do not run. Turn around, face the ghost, and as he comes near you, slap these potent ashes on to his face. He will run away and never bother you again!" The boy was still a little doubtful and apprehensive but the Swami reassured him many times to strengthen his faith.

Next day the boy arrived very happy, beaming with a smile. "It worked!" he said. "The ashes from your fire are really potent."

"Tell me how it went," the Swami asked.

"Well," replied the boy, "I carried the ashes in my hand and when the ghost came down from the tree, I remembered your advice. I did not run. I turned around, faced the ghost, and as he came near to grab me I slapped the ashes squarely on his face. He turned, ran, and vanished!"

The Swami said, "Really, now are you sure it was the ghost and not someone else whom you slapped?"

The boy was indeed very sure. The swami took out a little mirror from his bundle, showed it to the young lad who saw that the mark of five fingers with ashes was on his own face!

This parable is used to illustrate that the objects of

all our fears are projections from our own persons, and no other ghosts chase after us through evening's dark shadows in the woods. Furthermore, the only secret of happiness is that we should never try to escape from whatever we are most afraid of. As we turn around and face that which is chasing after us, it will turn tail and vanish.

Fear of death is more fearsome than death itself. Train the body without attachment, to accomplish its purpose but never forget that it is only a transient's nest. Strive for the realization of the true Self, that is, the unborn and undying life-force, *atman*. When one lives in full awareness of this true Self, there is no more meaning to the word death. The bird flies freely away from one night's perch: its freedom of wings is a joy and the infinite sky is not a source of fear.

The yogi knows this joy in infinity through careful processes of conquest over various systems within the personality, he masters the process of death itself. Until such mastery has been attained, we still have recourse to (1) the path of purifying our karma through right knowledge, thought, word and deed, and (2) by dying to our physical self daily in deep meditation, which is the awareness of the pure, immortal, spiritual Self that "I am."

Apa mrtyum jayati ya evam veda
He who knows thus, vanquishes the death away.

Appendix

Below we name some great classics in the world literature on the subject of death:

The most beautiful hymns and dialogues on the subject of death are found in the Vedic literature. The present-day liturgy of the last rites is also derived from these. I had intended to translate these Vedic hymns here but during the process of writing also discovered an exciting publication which has already accomplished this. I insist that the reader look through pages 540-610 of

The Vedic Experience: Mantra-manjari, An Anthology of the Vedas for Modern Man and Contemporary Celebration, a scholarly work, yet full of true insight, by Raimundo Panikkar, published from the University of California Press. Excluding some of the archaic rites, which were of limited usage even in 1500 B.C., the rest of the text will inspire the reader to learn to go across death as though on a bridge over a beautiful river. I also refer the reader to passages on deathlessness and immortality translated in the same anthology.

Katha Upanishad (approximately 1200-700 B.C.) presents a modified version of the earlier story, found in Taittiriya Brahmana. The text describes the journey of Nachiketas to the house of Death, who teaches the young sage the secrets of death and the ways of immortality. Numerous translations of this Upanishad are available. The reader is especially referred to H. H. Swami Rama's *Life Here and Hereafter* published by the Himalayan Institute.

Garuda-Purana, (approximately 400B.C. - 400 A.D.), describes in detail the laws of karma in terms of the soul's journeys through heavenly, infernal and mundane existences. Couched in a highly mystical language, the work has not yet been translated into English.

Egyptian Book of the Dead, and various other pyramid inscriptions, are well known but their symbolism is lost in antiquity. No living tradition of the Egyptian priests has survived unless the Hermetic, Gnostic, Coptic and similar schools may be suspected of having absorbed some of the teaching. There are only a few passages that clearly indicate a yoga-like awareness or may speak of the modern mind. We have left the Egyptian Book for a future discussion.

Tibetan Book of the Dead, about which Carl Jung has said; "For years (this work) has been my constant companion, and to it I owe not only many stimulating ideas and discoveries, but also many fundamental insights."

Had not living tradition continued, the symbolism of the Tibetan Book would have been as obscure today as that of the Egyptian Book. Tibet, however, formed a part of the Himalayan chain and we yet have living masters who can not only explain but can lead a few chosen disciples across the shores of death. For a glimpse of these Masters' *siddhis* in this area, see Section XIII, pages 435-464 titled "Mastery Over Life and Death" in *Living with the Himalayan Masters*, published by the Himalayan Institute, written by H. H. Swami Rama.

Two translations of The *Tibetan Book of the Dead* are available: 1) Evans-Wentz, Oxford University Press, numerous editions, 2) Fremantle, Francesca and Chogyam Trungpa, Shambhala, 1975.

Pythagoras (6th century B.C.) believed in reincarnation. His teaching as presented by Ovid is summarized here.

Phaedo, the well-known last dialogue of Socrates dealing with immortality and reincarnation is summarized here.

Dante's *Divine Comedy* is a journey beyond death, giving us many inspiring passages, but for the purpose of our discussion we have not included its poetic speculation.

Here we are leaving out many passages of great import that are found in Sanskrit and other world literature, too numerous for this volume. Throughout history realized human beings, philosophers and poets have said much about the questions of death, reincarnation and immortality. Even more inspiring, and giving greater insight into the nature of death are the narratives of the last moments of those great beings. Where necessary to support our argument we have included in this work some quotations from: Head, Joseph and Cranston, S.L., *Re-incarnation: An East-West Anthology,* A Quest Book, 1975 and *Reincarnation, The Phoenix Fire Mystery*, Julian Press/Crown Publishers, New York, 1977. This is the most complete possible anthology on reincarnation, shedding light on the idea of death from the viewpoint of all great cultures, philosophies and traditions.

Specific to the Chinese and Japanese traditions on death the following works must be consulted: 1) Kapleau, Philip, *The Wheel of Death*, Harper and Row, 1971; 2) Stryk, Lucien and Nikimoto, Nakashi, *Zen Poems;* 3) *The Diamond Sutra and the Sutra of Hui Neng*, trans. Price, A. and Mou-Lam, Wong.

Dr. Raymond A. Moody's *Life After Life* and the work of Osis and Haraldsson as referred to by Daniel Goleman in an article titled "Back from the Brink" in *Psychology Today*, April, 1977, page 56, will be referred to in our discussion.

We were tempted to include in an appendix poems 86-102 in Rabindranath Tagore's *Gitanjali*. It creates a mood that is an antidote to the dread of death conveyed in the Psalms of David. The Psalms try to comfort us as we approach the shadows in the valley of death; *Gitanjali* makes us rejoice as we reach the peaks of a reunion with Light.

The work of such outstanding figures as Elisabeth Kubler-Ross and those who have published in her wake has been deliberately left out. We are trying here to understand the nature of death from a spiritual and experiential perspective. No one can counsel the dying, the anxious and the bereaved today without training in this area of counseling but currently professional thantology is powerless as to understanding the nature of death itself. For that we look to guidance from the yogis of the Himalayas.

Himalayan Institute Publications

Book of Wisdom (Ishopanishad)	Swami Rama
A Call to Humanity	Swami Rama
Choosing a Path	Swami Rama
Enlightenment Without God	Swami Rama
Freedom from the Bondage of Karma	Swami Rama
Inspired Thoughts of Swami Rama	Swami Rama
Lectures on Yoga	Swami Rama
Life Here and Hereafter	Swami Rama
Living with the Himalayan Masters	Swami Rama
Love Whispers	Swami Rama
Path of Fire and Light, Vol. I	Swami Rama
Path of Fire and Light, Vol. II	Swami Rama
Perennial Psychology of the Bhagavad Gita	Swami Rama
A Practical Guide to Holistic Health	Swami Rama
Creative Use of Emotion	Swami Rama, Swami Ajaya
Science of Breath	Swami Rama, Rudolph Ballentine, M.D., Alan Hymes, M.D.
Yoga and Psychotherapy	Swami Rama, Rudolph Ballentine, M.D., /Swami Ajaya
Yoga-sutras of Patanjali	Usharbudh Arya, D.Litt.
Superconscious Meditation	Usharbudh Arya, D.Litt.
Mantra and Meditation	Usharbudh Arya, D.Litt.
Philosophy of Hatha Yoga	Usharbudh Arya, D.Litt.
Meditation and the Art of Dying	Usharbudh Arya, D.Litt.
God	Usharbudh Arya, D.Litt.
Psychotherapy East and West: A Unifying Paradigm	Swami Ajaya, Ph.D.
Yoga Psychology	Swami Ajaya, Ph.D.
Psychology East and West	Swami Ajaya, Ph.D. (ed.)
Diet and Nutrition	Rudolph Ballentine, M.D.
Transition to Vegetarianism	Rudolph Ballentine, M.D.
Theory and Practice of Meditation	Rudolph Ballentine, M.D. (ed.)
Freedom from Stress	Phil Nuernberger, Ph.D.
Science Studies Yoga	James Funderburk, Ph.D.
Homeopathic Remedies	Drs. Anderson, Buegel, Chernin
Seven Systems of Indian Philosophy	Rajmani Tigunait, Ph.D.
Swami Rama of the Himalayas	L. K. Misra, Ph.D. (ed.)
The Quiet Mind	John Harvey, Ph.D. (ed.)
Meditation in Christianity	Himalayan Institute
Hatha Yoga Manual I	Samskrti and Veda
Hatha Yoga Manual II	Samskrti and Judith Franks

To order or to request a free mail order catalog call or write: The Himalayan Publishers, RR 1, Box 400. Honesdale, PA 18431. Toll-Free 1-800-444-5772